THE PUBLIC RAPING
OF RELIA UNION

Dr. Beverley R. Taylor

authorHOUSE®

AuthorHouse™
1663 Liberty Drive
Bloomington, IN 47403
www.authorhouse.com
Phone: 1-800-839-8640

First published by AuthorHouse 3/23/2010

ISBN: 978-1-4490-7522-4 (e)
ISBN: 978-1-4490-7520-0 (sc)
ISBN: 978-1-4490-7521-7 (hc)

Library of Congress Control Number: 2010900445

Printed in the United States of America
Bloomington, Indiana

This book is printed on acid-free paper.

While trying to make a decision regarding writing this book and boldly state the malfunctions of the system as I view them, I became fearful, fearful that I would anger someone. Then I recalled President Obama's campaign speeches where he stated… "We should be able to disagree without becoming disagreeable." This, along with the following quote I heard while attending Mass, gave me the strength that I needed to carry out my goal. It is most powerful read aloud:

"Fear imprisons…Faith liberates.
Fear paralyzes….Faith empowers.
Fear disheartens….Faith encourages.
Fear sickens…. Faith heals.
Fear makes useless….Faith makes serviceable.
And most of all…Fear puts hopelessness at the heart of life while faith rejoices in God."

Reverend Harry Emerson Fosdick (1878-1969)
Baptist Preacher and Pastor of the
First Presbyterian Church in New York.

DEDICATION

Dedicated in loving memory of Mrs. Aurelia C. Patterson, my mother, Reinhold, my husband, Reinhold, Jr. and Kody, my sons, Mrs. Faye A. Pointer, my cousin, and all the wonderful educators of the world.

ACKNOWLEDGEMENTS

I would like to express my gratitude to all the wonderful people who made it possible for me to complete this book. In particular I want to thank all the dedicated teachers and principals who take pride in helping our students succeed, especially four outstanding principals under whom I had the honor to serve: Mr. Arthur Hull, Mr. Willie McNeil, Mr. Wayne Finch, Dr. James Catchings, and my former supervisor Mrs. Faye Deanes. I also thank two school secretaries who always went beyond their duties to assist me and our students, Mrs. Gwendolyn Bowles and Mrs. Brown.

Next, I truly appreciate my partners in fitness, Ms. Mary F. Thomas, Ms. Odella McKinnon, Mrs. Dell Stiner, Mrs. Crystal Meeks, Dr. Joyce Freshwater, Mrs. Betty Sanders, Mrs. Rosiland Gilmore, Mrs. Blanche Wilson, Mrs. Shep Bachus, Mrs. Chanel Alnasan, and Mrs. Regina Bethel Williams, who for many, many years helped me to relieve the many stresses of modern day living. Also, I deeply appreciate my close friend, Mrs. Rita Kendrick, who looked closely at the final version of the book and offered suggestions for improvement.

I am further thankful for the following contributors: Mr. Cornelius Johnson for his sincere interest, encouragement, and valuable information; Mrs. Ladawna Byars for sharing her outstanding creativity during the development of the novel and providing stimulating suggestions; Mrs. Marcella Reekie for serving as my technical editor and providing much appreciated guidance and advice; Mrs. Wilma Black-Moore for serving as my manuscript editor; Father John Geaney, my pastor, and my pew buddies,

Mrs. Evelyn M. McNeal-Harris, Mrs. Raye P. Dudley, Mrs. Audrey Parker McGhee, Mrs. Theris Horne Adair and Mrs. Evelyn Vavansseur for their spiritual support.

Especially, my appreciation goes to Ms. Venita Martin who believed in me and fought long and hard for the protection of my constitutional rights. I am thankful to President Obama and Mrs. Obama for serving as positive parent role models and for sharing with the world that all children deserve to be number one in their parents' lives and nothing or no-one should come before our children's physical, mental, and educational needs.

I am deeply indebted to my husband Reinhold, whose extraordinary intellect is matched by his patience, love, and understanding. I give thanks to my two sons Reinhold, Jr. and Kody and my cousin Mrs. Faye Pointer for their support and encouragement. I am thankful to my good friends and co-workers, Dr. Shirley Hilliard and Mrs. Myrtle Malone for always being there for me; My cousins, Mr. Carl and Ms. Michelle Flake for always willing to give me a helping hand.

I truly appreciate the efficient service I received from all the wonderful Librarians at Memphis Public Libraries and Information Center.

TABLE OF CONTENTS

Introduction

"Do you know how many people have been wronged by an employer?" Attorney Elderman said. The difference is most of them didn't have the guts to do anything about it. You did. This was a major accomplishment for you, and I'm just glad that I was able to be a part of it."

"Okay so if you'll just sign right here, it'll be over. All those years of dealing with this and it comes down to your signature. It must've been really hard. I mean, it's been tough for me, and I'm not even the one who went through it all. I can't imagine what these past seven years have been like for you. But anyway, I'm just glad we were able to get what was due to you." I watched her lips move and couldn't help but want to shove each word back down her throat. I wanted to scream, "What was due? I know you don't think that this is all I'm due! These were the words that I wanted to scream! But no words came out when my mouth opened.

"Maybe you're right. I should take it huh?"

"I think so. But that's just my professional opinion; the final decision is yours to make."

The settlement was in front of me. My hands and body were shaking as the pen anchored between my fingers. I always thought that having judgment in my favor would automatically heal the wounds that were left behind. Now, as I sat and stared at the dollar amount that some random decider of justice assigned to my pain, I was certain that this would in no way lead to my healing. It wasn't just about me. It was more about my duty what I felt I owed society to ensure that the assault would stop here, and that no child would lose a piece of himself or herself in the forsaken hole of a system that we call education. I lifted the pen and attempted to sign, but my hand just wouldn't move. Instead, my mind raced and my heart pounded as memories of my struggle surfaced...

Chapter 1   A Public Raping

Her arms were pinned down tightly on the desk. A well-groomed Caucasian man in a tan suit held one arm down while an African American woman held down the other arm. They laughed cynically as they watched their partner in crime invade every inch of her tiny frame. Her tear-stained face told of her struggle as she fought with all her might, trying desperately to free herself from their grip. They seemed amused by her. She fought as if her life depended on it. Their mouths moved in laughter yet no sound escaped from their lips. She heard nothing.

She paid close attention to her surroundings trying to take in as many details as she could. She saw a chalkboard, lots of desks, children's pictures and the ABCs posted on the wall. Around her, people stood and watched as if nothing out of the ordinary was going on. Some sipped from their morning cups of coffee; others graded papers. Some sat in what appeared to be planning parent/teacher meetings, while others signed paperwork and shook hands in casual conversation. No one objected to the invasion that was taking place before their eyes. How could they watch? Why didn't anyone call for help? She knew they saw it. How could anyone ignore the bruising and the beating that she was enduring?

Insult added to injury as the assaulters switched places with each other, and the rape began all over again. Over and over, they probed her intimate places and left scar after scar, smudge after smudge, quickly erasing the confidence that she once had. The horrified woman searched desperately for the strength to fight and the will to remain conscious. As fatigue grew, she vowed not to give in and to go down fighting--even if it killed her...

CHAPTER 1

I tapped my foot in excitement while I waited for my name to be called. Years of training, education, hard work, and, of course, winning the "Counselor Excellence Award" led me to this moment. I felt prepared and couldn't wait to show the interview committee just how prepared I was. "Mrs. Union, they're ready for you now."

I stood and gave myself one last look over to ensure that everything was in place and that I had no glaring wardrobe "malfunctions". I sported a conservative navy blue suit, complete with a white blouse, and navy shoes. A stickler for details, I had made certain that everything was perfect down to my accessories of pearl earrings, necklace and a matching bracelet. I decided not to remind the young lady of my proper title. I had spent years away from my family to earn the esteemed title of Dr. Relia Union, but it just wasn't the right time to make a big deal about it. It was the time to shine.

The doors of the conference room swung open revealing a tough crowd. I held my head high with confidence and took my place at the head of the table. My comfort began to waiver a little when I took notice of the people and aura that filled the room. Clara Thomas, Supervisor of Social Services, sat directly across from me. She eyed me carefully at first, then almost disdainfully. I initially dismissed the reaction as my imagination playing tricks on me and attempted to shake off the nervous pressure that I was obviously under. For about 2 minutes, I quietly and anxiously anticipated the first question. No one spoke. They all just sat very still and watched me as if to gauge my body language. To my left was Dr. Madeoff, Pre- School-12 Children's Services Coordinator; Cindy Lewis, a fellow counselor, sat on the right of me. The panel consisted of three African Americans and four Caucasians. Just when the silence was becoming unbearable, the first question was raised. "So Dr. Union, could you please tell us just a little about yourself and why you think you would be a good fit for this position?"

"Yes, I attained my Doctorate in Curriculum, Instruction and Policy Study. I have achieved the highest counseling level that can be earned by a counselor. Our State Board of Health Related Boards under the division of Professional Counselors and Marital & Family Therapists has awarded me the title of Certified Professional Counselor, and I am also certified by our State Board of Education as a School Counselor. I have more than 20 years of experience in counseling, administration, and teaching. During those 20 years, I've gained experience in parenting programs, community involvement, career awareness programs, individual, classroom and small group counseling and guidance programs, and curriculum development. In my opinion, a position such as this one would require someone who has worked in a variety of roles and shown evidence of success. I have served as a substitute teacher, a classroom teacher, a school counselor, acting director of counseling and acting principal, and an adjunct professor, where I taught counseling and administrative courses. I strongly believe because of the various roles that I have fulfilled that the time has arrived for me to move into a new and more challenging role."

"Uhm- hum," Dr. Madeoff mumbled somewhat as she made a short notation on her pad. "This position calls for administrative experience. Can you please tell us of any administrative experience that you have? How did it prepare you for a role such as this one?"

"Yes. As I just previously mentioned and if you noticed on my résumé, I have served as both acting principal and acting director. In these roles, I was expected to make decisions in ill-defined situations just as an administrator is expected to do.

"Acting principal? How long did you do that? A day? What, two at the most?"

"No, actually it was much more extensive than that. I was left in charge any time my principal and assistant principal were off campus. The duration lasted over five years, which is also about as long as I was acting director. My director requested in her absent that I answer any questions or concerns that my co-counselors would have regarding our counseling program. I was often given the role of mentor for those up and coming counselors. While serving in this capacity, I was able to test my abilities in crisis management, conflict resolution, and problem solving. It was a great learning experience, and a very big part of my preparation for this role."

"What kind of crisis did you run into?"

"Excuse me. Could you please repeat your question?"

"Crisis. You said that you tested your abilities in the areas of crisis management, problem solving, and conflict resolution. You did say that, right?"

"Yes. I did."

"So, what kind of crisis did you manage?" I was taken aback. I looked at Dr. Madeoff for a second and studied the harsh expression on her face. I looked for her eyes to soften and for the tension in the room to dissipate. Instead, her glare seemed to intensify when we made eye contact. Something wasn't right in this room; the air was thick, and the knot in my throat grew as each mocking tick of the clock on the wall passed. I refused to believe that what I was feeling was real. Dr. Madeoff was the same person who had supported me in my nomination for a prestigious counseling award. I couldn't wrap my mind around the possibility that she was really acting so horribly. It had to be me. My overwhelming desire to earn this position had to be the source of this anxiety. "Do you need me to repeat the question?"

"No, thank you." I brushed the tension away and focused in on my goal. I deserved that job, and I was determined to show this panel why. "There were several problematic occurrences that I experienced as acting principal. One that particularly stands out-"

"I asked you for an example of a crisis, not a problematic occurrence."

"Yes. If I may complete my response, I think I can give you several examples of such."

"Oh, go on."

"One incident that stands out as a problematic occurrence was the very heated discussion that a teacher had with a parent. They came very close to having a physical altercation, and I was serving as the acting principal at the time. I not only had to diffuse the argument, I also had to document the incident and the action pursued. Also, I think one of the major crises that I experienced as acting principal came recently, when it was discovered that one of our students was being physically assaulted on a regular basis by a family member. It became a crisis once it was discovered that the abuse had occurred in the school parking lot on more than one occasion. My response had to be within policy but also had to give special attention to the fragile needs of the child. I'm proud to say that once my principal returned, there was very little left for her to do in this situation. I try to perform at a level of excellence that takes a huge load off my peers as well as those whom I report to. My principals often describe me as a team player." The room remained silent as a couple of interviewers made diligent notations on their notepads.

"Dr. Union, what would you say is the major thing that you've done to increase parent involvement?" That was the question I was waiting on. During my career, parental involvement was a large part of my platform. I honestly felt that I could answer this one in my sleep. The response flowed fluently from my lips with pride and confidence. I ran down the list of award-winning programs that I'd organized over the years and the many extra initiatives where I had given my time and energy simply for the sake of my students. "I firmly believe that learning starts at home. I made sure that my parents felt comfortable any time they were invited to conferences, workshops or meetings. I began each school year with a parental need assessment and finished the year with a parental survey. I put forth great effort to insure that I had fulfilled their needs. I designed and developed a parent resource room that I filled with valuable information regarding school and home. I have held countless parent meetings, conferences and workshops. My Mentor Program that placed more than 50 mentors with at risk students gave my single parents a big helping hand. The impact that the mentors had on their students was amazing. That alone brought in many parents who were interested in getting their child a mentor.

I wrote and received a $12,000 grant. This money paid for career awareness materials for use by the students as well as their parents. Through the City Literacy Program, I provided award winning books to those primary students whose parents could not afford to purchase such celebrated titles. The program enabled the parents to read and converse with their young children. This in turn increased our students' academic progress. I also worked closely with our parent advocate to make sure that our parents were provided with transportation to parent conferences, meetings, and their children's doctor appointments. Those are only a few examples of the things I've done to increase parental involvement. Should I continue?"

"Is that ALL YOU DID?" asked Cindy Lewis whose question carried the sting of a salted wound and sent waves of shock down my spine. "Excuse me?" I responded, genuinely surprised.

"Is that all you did? If parental involvement truly was a major part of your platform, then it would seem that you would have more examples, or should I say examples that carried more of an impact." I sat still and wondered if my expression gave any hint of what I was feeling on the inside. I felt betrayed, stunned, and displaced. The betrayal came from my realization that the person whom I thought was one of my biggest supporters appeared to be purposefully sabotaging my interview. She sat and stared at me with venomous eyes. If looks could kill, my fate would surely have been sealed.

"Well, what I gave you was a few of many examples. If you would like, I can give several more with the same amount of detail with which I gave the others. The important thing that I would like to go on record for having stated is this: Just as parental involvement has been a major part of my approach thus far, if selected for this role, I will continue to pursue it with creativity."

"I also developed and coordinated The Career Awareness and Tutoring Program. The Program had two objectives. The first was to help students to see the relationship between school and a career. The second was to provide tutorial services to those students in kindergarten through grade three who needed help with basic skills. In this program, students who were in grades 4-6 went through a formal selection process to get a job as a tutor. There were postings, applications, and required references. The students actually entered the world of work. This was accomplished by allowing them to experience all the components such as being hired, fired, laid off and promoted. Students who were hired tutored the kindergarten through third grade and were paid for doing so. The money for students' salary came by way of a grant that I wrote. My Career Programs brought many resource people into the schools to inform students about unusual careers or those careers that students did not know existed."

"Okay," Lewis's quick one word response reeked of disinterest. The audacity of some of the interviewers stunned me. Here they sat, perfectly placed in positions not based on their qualifications, but on socialization. It was their acquaintance not their performance, that afforded them this opportunity. They sat in judgment of me. It was frustrating because some had failed to complete the minimum requirements for the positions they held. Whether it was the lack of classroom teaching experience, or the lack of certification, several of my condemners sat naked in judgment of me, flaws glaring and claws bearing. Still, I held my composure and listened closely for the next question. Most of them did not own a knowledge base of counseling, nor did they have a sense of the needs of our children. How would they know which candidate was best for this extremely important position?

The rest of the interview was a bit of a blur. Those on the panel representing my peers listened carefully and wore thoughtful expressions. Throughout the interview, they too shifted in discomfort at the tension in the room and the hostile line of questioning. Finally, Dr. Madeoff gave me a strange look and said, "Well, Thank you Dr. Union. We will contact you after we have made our final decision." I stood and awkwardly let myself out without so much as a nod from several of the interviewers. As I passed, some of them smiled slyly as if they knew something that I didn't. I walked confidently and in victory because in my heart I too had a secret. This job was mine. The many years of hard work and dedication had prepared me for it, my prayers and constant contact with God dictated it, and as I exited the firing squad battered but not bruised, I claimed it.

Later that evening, Alexander and I discussed the panel interview over dinner. He was just as disbelieving as I was about their behavior. "Are you sure that you weren't imagining it? I mean, maybe it was all of the excitement. You have been kind of anxious about this position."

"That's what I was thinking at first, but it got worse towards the end. For some reason, I still can't shake this weird feeling that I have about all of this. I wish you could have been there. It was like a conspiracy or something. They were treating me as if I were the enemy."

"But you're still okay as far as getting the job right?"

"Oh yeah. I'm still confident about the position. I was just caught off guard by the whole thing. The panel that they had didn't really represent the needs of the position well. Only two of the members had ever worked as elementary counselors. Even Dr. Madeoff doesn't have the degrees or any experience working with young developing children. I'm just curious about why there wasn't better representation. I know of three outstanding elementary counselors and two excellent elementary retired supervisors who could have served on the interview panel. They were qualified and available, yet they weren't selected for the interview panel. In fact, some of them said that they requested to be a member of the panel. I don't get it. You should have seen Cindy Lewis. She was the worst. You know how I've been working on all these ideas to increase parental activity?"

"Yeah, you had over half of my office staff being mentors, including Addison and me. As much as you talk about it, I could've answered that question for you."

"Right. So when they asked me what I've done to increase parental involvement, I was excited. I knew that I had that one down pat. I went through my little spiel, and before I could finish my sentence, she sneers, *'Is that all you did?'* I couldn't believe it. The principal and the psychologist looked just as shocked as I did. I think they felt a little sorry for me. It was so unprofessional."

"Yeah. That is a little weird. At least you got it out of the way. The hard part is done. Now all you have to do is sit back and wait on your offer."

"I'm not sure if the hard part is over or not. I hope it is." Though the conversation subsided and the dinner conversation shifted to the boys and small talk, the interview remained at the forefront of my thoughts. My confidence in being awarded the position never wavered, but I honestly felt somewhat unnerved by the hostility.

Were there people in the room who didn't want me in this position? If so, why didn't they want me to have it? I'd given years of dedication to this school system, focused on making sure I was certified in all the right areas, and continuously developed my knowledge base so that when the time came for me to move to a position that demanded greater responsibility, I would be prepared. The time had come, and my uneasiness rested in not knowing whether all of my hard work would pay off.

It wasn't long before my anxiety about the interview for director died down. After nights of prayer and increased reassurance by my colleagues, I felt renewed and prepared to walk into this new experience. A couple of weeks passed, and I had come to the point where I answered every phone call on the first ring in anticipation of the "offer". Today's call was no different. "Good afternoon, Dr. Union." I answered in my professional tone.

"Hello Dr.Union. This is Dr.Madeoff. I was calling you about the director position."

"Oh great. I was hoping I would hear something soon."

"Well, we have run into an unfortunate situation, and we had to eliminate that posting. We did, however, take care of the administrative issues that were responsible for the position being eliminated. Because we had to do a completely new job posting, we are required to start the selection process all over again. I wanted to call you personally and give you the first opportunity to resubmit for this new position."

"Are there any differences between this position and the previous one?"

"No, the requirements, responsibilities, and pay grade are the same. It's just a new posting."

"Okay," I answered somewhat disappointed yet relieved that they thought enough of me to call and inform me personally. "So what's the next step?"

"Well, as I said earlier, this is a new posting, so we are starting the selection process all over. So you would simply go through the same process that you went through for the first one."

"So, I need to submit my résumé again?"

"Yes."

"And a new interview?"

"Unfortunately so. Is that going to be a problem?"

"No, not at all. Just inform me of my time for the interview, and I will be there. Thanks for calling."

"You're welcome. I appreciate your understanding."

"You're welcome." I hung up the phone and sat perfectly still for a second. I was feeling mixed emotions about the whole thing. Trying not to give it too much thought, I grabbed my purse and left the office for the day. It took me about 30 minutes to drive home.

"Hey honey," I cheerfully greeted my husband upon entering my house. "You're not going to believe what happened today."

"You got the call?"

"Yeah I got a call all right. They told me that the position that I interviewed for had been eliminated."

"What!"

"But, they were able to get permission to repost the same job-just under a new posting number."

"So… what does that mean?"

"It means that I have to apply all over again and do the interview all over too."

"Ahh," he responded, simply unsure of how to react. "Well, I guess it could have been worse. They could have eliminated the position completely."

"Yeah. I guess. But that first interview was rough. I'm not really looking forward to doing it over again, especially if I have to deal with the same people."

"Well, let's look at it on the bright side. If it's a new posting, you'll probably have a whole new interview panel. So not only did you get to wow the first group, you get a whole new group of people to highly impress…"

He answered as he pulled me into a reassuring embrace. I couldn't help but smile as my partner danced around me with the grace of an ox. He danced my way, took my briefcase off my shoulder and stared deep into my eyes. I knew exactly what his stare meant. Behind, it was an amazing emotion that he'd told me about on more than one occasion.

I remembered the first time he shared it with me. It was shortly after we were married that he had let me in on this intimate thought, "Sometimes…," he spoke tearfully, "if I watch you long enough, I almost forget that you're my wife. It's like the beauty that I see in you sometimes amazes me, and makes me wish that I could have the honor of making your acquaintance. Then just when I begin to long to know the woman behind that face, you smile. The want goes away, and all of a sudden, I feel overcome by thankfulness that you are not just an acquaintance, but also my other half. That's when the reality of my life with you blows me away."

Alexander Union and I had a very special kind of love. Since the first day of the first semester of my first year in college, we'd been in love. We married early and fought hard to overcome the obstacles that often came with young love. Though we'd seen some tough days, there was never a moment where either of us doubted the commitment that we shared. He watched me give birth to his sons and often said that he admired my strength, "…just like you blow me away every time you take another step to pursue your dreams."

I snapped back into the moment and tried to focus on what Alexander was saying. "Relia, don't allow this stuff to discourage you. You know what you can do, and they know it too. It just may take a little longer than you expected. You've waited this long; what's another couple of weeks?"

As it happened, because the first few steps were just a formality, the next interview came up very quickly. Within a week, my résumé was reviewed, and I received the notification of my interview date and time. Though I had been confident in my first interview nevertheless, I used it as a study guide in preparing for this one.

Walking into the room created an eerie feeling of déjà vu. It was the same room, same conference table, but a different interview panel. Where the previous interview team had seven members, this one had five. The team, which consisted of only one African American, differed drastically from the team of four whites and three African Americans that I had faced for the first interview. Once again, the disinterest on a few of the faces in the room immediately set the tone for the interview.

"Hello Dr. Union. I appreciate you coming in again. Clara Thomas was also scheduled to attend this interview; however, she is ill today and will be unable to join us." Dr. Madeoff introduced the rest of the panel quickly before rushing into the actual questioning. The panel consisted of an elementary principal who was a former counselor; Amy Folder's former child advocate; Cindy Lewis, who served on the first interview panel; and a friend of Cindy. I answered the questions clearly and was sure to carefully articulate my responses. Much to my disappointment, the parental involvement question did not come up. On more than one occasion, I noticed the team members shifting, as if they were bored. Once it was over, I stood and carefully studied the expression of each person in the room. None of them made eye contact with me; rather they sorted their papers uncomfortably and waited for the door to close behind me.

I carried thoughts of the interview with me to dinner. "So were they rude?"

"No. I wouldn't call it rude."

"Okay…so what would you call it?"

"Indifference. I could be wrong, but I got the feeling that they couldn't have cared less about anything that I had to say. At least in the first interview I knew they were listening. Sure, they were rude and unprofessional about it, but at least they heard me. I'm not sure if those people heard or cared about a word that I had to say." I picked over my food, too consumed with my thoughts to enjoy the meal. Alexander sat across from me and said nothing. His expression was that of concern. "I just don't get it. It's as if the very people who have been telling me over and over again how great a job I've been doing, sat in that room and betrayed me not once but twice."

"Wait baby. Don't jump the gun now. You don't know for sure that they betrayed you. They may have just felt bad about the last interview and wanted to tone things down a bit. You don't know how they scored you. I still say that you have nothing to worry about."

"I know. I guess I was just expecting something different. There were only five people on this panel, and only one of them was African American. The last one had seven people, and three of them were African Americans. I don't understand why they chose people who didn't have the experience needed for this position to interview me. Most members of this panel did not have the experience of working with our students. It appeared that they just pulled names out of the air and gave them some questions to ask whose answers they did not know.

"What about Lewis? Was she cool?"

"Too cool if you ask me. She went from drilling me last time to rushing me through this time. I couldn't even finish one question before they were shoving the next one down my throat."

"Were they taking notes?"

"No. I mean, yes. I guess, shoot I don't know. All I know is the last interview lasted about an hour, and this one was no more than 20 minutes. It was the same job, same room, same conference table, but a completely different interview."

"Okay let's just relax. You already know that you're well-qualified for the job. Relia, it'll be okay. I promise."

"Thank you baby, I know." I allowed the conversation to change to how Alexander's day went and even participated in the conversation as if he was the only thing on my mind. Yet I was actually still bothered by how things seemed to be playing out. Deep inside, I prayed that Alexander's faith in me would not be misplaced.

Chapter 2   Wake Up Call

By now, the stares were beginning to burn. She watched as they inched closer to her, hiding ill intentions behind deceitful smiles. She walked quickly, eyeing the door that represented her safe space. If she could just make it into her classroom, she'd be safe. Relief washed over her when the doorknob to her room turned, and she stepped over the threshold. She peaked out through the little square window, seeing no-one. It's as if they'd all vanished into thin air. Unsure of whether to be relieved or concerned, she turned and decided to go on about her day.

The audience that she faced startled her. Instead of her normal class of students, she was greeted by the same faces that she'd just left on the other side of the door. Everybody was doing their own thing, as if she was the least of their concerns. The atmosphere was eerie. Unsure of how to approach the situation, she picked up her planner and pen and sat down at her desk. Every attempt to concentrate was useless; her thoughts escaped her. Fear crawled down her spine and radiated into her fingertips causing them to nervously tap on the desk.

The ring leader stepped forward and placed an apple in her lap, brushing her leg as he pulled his hand back. Chills danced up her spine as she stood and allowed the apple to fall to the floor. The chatter in the room started as a hush and quickly grew until the noise began to hinder her ability to think. Slowly another stood, this time a woman, and walked to her. She extended her hands and opened them allowing an object to fall to the floor. The fearful woman flinched in expectation of the crash. It made no sound. Things began to make even less sense as the object lying on the floor came into view. It was her degree, straight from the mantel of her home, now lying on the floor at their feet.

As if it were choreographed, each person in the room stood and walked in her direction. Their steps were slow and deliberate, silent and almost morbid. Danger began to feel imminent, the air thickened, and before she knew it...

CHAPTER 2

I tried to maintain a "business as usual" approach to working in the days that followed the interviews. Confident that an offer would soon come, I made every attempt to give the same effort to my current position that I always had. However, the excitement led to anxiousness, which led to nervousness, which led to distraction. Nevertheless, it was particularly important to stay focused because I was on the tail end of one of my biggest projects. We were only weeks away from implementing my Dental Hygiene Program. The time that I'd put into working towards the director position had been quite a task--months of planning and managing.

Planning the project had been tedious at best. In the beginning I tried to log all my phone calls, but as we got closer and closer to the Dental Hygiene Program, the logging was time-consuming.

"Can you confirm for me what services you will be offering?"

"Prophy, oral exams,and sealants."

"And you will bring all of the equipment? Is there anything I need to provide?"

"Yes Ma'am. All you need to bring are the students."

"Wow! You have no idea how excited I am about this. We have students who have never been to the dentist before. When researching the program, I hoped that someone would see how life changing this could be for some of our students. I'm so glad that everyone came together to make this happen for them."

"I know. We consider it a blessing to be of service to our community. We are extremely thankful for all of your help. Most people don't want to be bothered with the extra work required."

"Well, is there anything else that I can do for you?"

"No Ma'am. Not right now. I'll call you a couple of days before just to make sure that everything is in order."

"Okay. Thanks again. Talk to you then!" I hung up the phone feeling so very proud of how things were shaping up.

It had been a couple of weeks since my interview, and the excitement of the new position was still fresh in my mind. I came home eager to share some of my new ideas with Alexander. After pulling in my driveway, I checked the mailbox as I normally did. "Junk, junk, bill..."

My heart skipped a beat when I read the return address on the last piece of mail that was from the school system. It seemed like enough time had passed for the offer to be made, but I had assumed that a verbal offer would come first. In my regular routine, I would take the mail in and place it on the kitchen counter. Sometime after dinner, I would get around to reading those items that I felt were relevant; this one, though, could not wait.

"Thank you for your interest in the director position. While your qualities and dedication as a counselor are definitely appreciated, we regret to inform you that Amy Folder was offered and has since accepted the position. We hope that you will continue to look for areas of growth within our School System." The words hit me like the force of a train. Only this train was silent, slamming me right in the face. Speechless, I turned my key and let myself into the house. Something in my mind was telling me that this wasn't real. It was as if my short-term memory was failing, and the words on the letter somehow were insensible. My heart pounded in my throat as a wave of heat rushed over my entire body. I sat down at the kitchen table and read the entire letter again, concentrating on every single word on the page. I took the envelope in my hand and read the addressee information as well as the return label.

By the time Alexander made it home, the news had begun to sink in. I was just about done preparing a quick meal when he walked in the door. "Hey baby." He came in with that same greeting every day. He wasn't an excitable man, so his hello was always the same and far from a telling sign of how much he missed me. "Hey," I replied, with a shaky and weak voice. I, on the other hand, the exact opposite of Alexander, carried my emotions on my sleeve; he could tell something was wrong from the way I said hello. He paused and immediately inquired, "Is every thing okay?"

"Not really. I got the news about the job today."

"And?"

"And I didn't get it."

"What do you mean you didn't get it? Are they not filling that position?"

"I mean, I didn't get the job. Yeah they filled it all right; they offered it to someone else, and she accepted it." Alexander stood there as if he wanted to support me, but was unsure of how to do it. He reached out and pulled me into a comforting reassuring hug; I allowed it but did not reciprocate. He held me there until he felt me relax a little and some of the tension dissipated. "Okay, let me finish this dinner so we can eat," I interrupted the hug and went back to preparing dinner.

"Baby, you don't have to cook. We can go grab a bite. That way you can just relax."

"I'm about done, so really, it's no big deal." I moved quickly around the kitchen, trying to avoid eye contact. "Besides, why would we go out when we have nothing to celebrate?"

"Who said anything about celebrating? I was talking about eating. Let's just get out of the house and go to a nice restaurant and talk about whatever you're feeling."

"Who said I was feeling anything?"

"Well, I'm sure you're feeling something. You had your heart set on this position. But even if you don't want to talk about it, we can still eat. The most important thing is that you are able to relax."

"I'm just saying, we have no reason to go out to dinner. We're here; the food is here, so let's just eat." I slammed the silverware down on the table as my irritation grew. "Please."

"Right, let's just eat." It was obvious that Alexander didn't know what to make of my behavior. Inside, I felt ashamed for taking my frustration out on him. He didn't deserve it, and I knew it. Yet, I still didn't apologize. Instead, I tried to soften my tone and compose myself for a meal with Alexander and our youngest son, Roman.

Roman was a med student and a product of our school system. He contradicted the common perception that a public school education was inferior and unable to produce quality results. After attending public schools from kindergarten through high school, Roman attended a well-known university and medical school on full scholarships. With every Christmas break that passed, I realized that we were closer and closer to the day that he would be completely on his own. It had come to the point where Alexander and I valued these small conversations at dinner.

I tried to act as normally as I possibly could during dinner. I tried to keep my professional worries and concerns invisible to our two sons.

Though they were both adults, there was still a certain side to "mom" that they just hadn't seen. It wasn't the time to share that sometimes hard work and education didn't exactly pay off. Instead, we remained attentive to our youngest as he talked about his day. As a med school student, Roman had enough of his own worries, and we prided ourselves in being attentive to each one. He talked often about his classes and how some of his classmates often worried whether the schooling could prepare them for the "real thing."

"You know what I mean? They teach you all of these facts, and we take test after test. Before you know it, you're in residency. As doctors, we can't afford to get it wrong. One mistake can mean that someone loses a mother, father, or child. But, I'm okay for the most part. I think it's the way that they allow us to get hands on experience while we are learning that makes me confident."

"Roman, you're doing well. You're making good grades and your evaluations are excellent. I know you'll be ready. Your school is known for producing outstanding doctors. They are going to make sure that you're well-prepared before you enter a hospital."

"I guess. My classmates and I always talk about that. What if the whole education thing isn't all that you need? And what if we don't have those other factors that it takes to succeed? I know I can do this, and I'm going to make a good doctor, but if it takes more than just education, I can't say the same for all of my classmates." I sat quietly and listened to the conversation between Alexander and Roman. I'd usually be the first one to offer a cute, little inspirational anecdote. Today, however, I stood on the sidelines. My situation may have been an example of education not being enough. My son could not have known that his concerns were familiar ones to me. What's worse is that from the look of things, his concerns were not only real but also valid.

After dinner, I made sure that nothing about my routine changed. I cleared the table and cleaned the kitchen, stopping every once in a while to answer a question or two from Alexander. It wasn't until after the house was silent and I was alone with my thoughts that I opened up my mind and allowed my emotions to come in. The living room was dark and rain pelted ever so softly against the window pane. I sprawled out on the sofa and began to wallow in emotion. I replayed both interviews over and over in my mind, switching the point-of-view to different perspectives. Each and every word I analyzed; every expression I studied. No matter how many times I changed the perspective, I kept coming up with the same answer: failure. I had failed to deliver; I had failed to perform. After all my so-called education and dedication, I had failed to succeed.

What was it all for? I had left my children and my husband and gone three states away to pursue my doctorate. Lonely days and sleepless nights were abundant while I studied. As I had waved good-bye to my family, I told myself that I was setting an example for my boys, that I was about to embark on a journey with an amazing destination. I was supposed to be their very own true to life and personal testimony of how hard work and education would open all doors. Yet, nothing about my career had changed since completing my doctorial work and giving over 20 years of dedicated professional service.

The letter about the director position caused feelings to come to the surface that I did not recognize. Was I selfish? Could I have possibly been so self-centered that I got sick to the stomach at the thought of someone being more deserving of this job than me? I always thought myself to be a strong believer in God's will and His timing; yet, as I sat and tried to free my mind from this feeling of failure, even that didn't help.

The tears ran faster than I could wipe them away, until finally I was fed up with chasing them. I looked around for something to console me and saw the bookcase. It held the key to who I really was. Each shelf represented a layer of Relia. On the first shelf, there were pictures of my boys, their honor diplomas, and trophies. They grew up to be wonderful men, and each one was a product of Alexander and me. As of now, they were both already showing signs of great potential. Roman was a very patient and gentle person. He will make a wonderful doctor because of those two characteristics. Addison was following in his father's foot steps and becoming a very successful business man. His wisdom reaches far beyond his chronological age.

The second shelf was full of fitness books and magazines, most of which had articles by me or about me. As the owner and operator of a fitness center, I'd become a pillar in my community and an expert in health and wellness. I had a fitness television show, and held numerous workshops for churches and health fairs. I was on the executive committee of one of our national women's health organizations and attended countless health conferences. Over the years, fitness had become as vital to me as the air I breathe. I set my sights on serving the community by educating people about the importance of fitness, and in turn, I gained more emotionally and spiritually than I could have ever expected. Nothing gave me more joy than watching women transform as they begin to give their bodies the attention that they deserve and leave the medication on the shelves of the pharmacists.

On the next shelf were milestones of my career development. Three degrees sat perfectly aligned on the shelf, with certifications and awards scattered amongst them, including, of course, my professional counseling license that only a few had ventured to obtain. I wanted so badly to run my hands along the shelves and knock everything off. I closed my eyes and attempted to familiarize myself with my own embarrassment. Before long, my mind settled into temporary rest followed by a night of tossing and turning on the sofa.

I awakened to the sound of Alexander preparing for work. My head pounded from a headache as I peaked through one eye, then the other. "What time is it?"

"About six; you were sleeping and I didn't want to disturb you, but I figured you might be late for work if I didn't get you up."

"I'm not going."

"What do you mean?"

"I don't feel well. I decided to stay home today."

"Okay. Relia, I love you. I know it seems tough right now, but it'll get better. I promise."

"I'll talk to you a little later."

"Bye babe."

Alexander kissed me on the cheek and walked away reluctantly. He could sense the trouble I was having. After the door closed, I rolled off the sofa and trudged to my bedroom. I plopped down on the bed, pulled the duvet over my head, and curled up in a fetal position. The sun was still hidden behind the cold winter clouds, and the bedroom was draped in gloominess. Sleep evaded me, yet I lay still, unable to leave the comfort of hiding. After what felt like 20 minutes, the phone rang. I rolled over slowly, determined to ignore the call. Alexander's name on the caller ID changed my mind, and I reluctantly picked the phone up.

"Hello."

"Hey, you feel any better?"

"Not really."

"What are you up to?"

"Lying here."

"Ohh," Alexander seemed surprised. "So do you need me to bring you anything? I can pick you up some lunch."

"Lunch?" His offer surprised me. "What time is it?"

"Just after one." Alexander spoke patiently. I couldn't believe how quickly the day had flown by. "No. Thanks for asking though. I'm not really hungry."

"Relia, I know this is hard. It's not the end of the world though. You are too strong to allow this setback to consume the woman that you are and shadow your accomplishments. You've done some amazing things, and you're an amazing woman. Don't you forget that."

"Right."

"No really baby. You are."

"Can you imagine what people will say? Look at the big shot doctor. She made this whole big deal of leaving her family, job, and home to go get her doctorate, always trying to be so committed, but what does she have to show for it? She's been in the same position for the last 20 years. Not a thing. I know if I were them I would be amused too."

"But you're not them. You're you. These are the people that you have spent your whole career supporting and interacting with. I'm sure they are just as surprised and disappointed as you are that you didn't get it. You are being harder on yourself than you need to be."

"I just don't get it Alexander. How can a person give all that I have given and not be hurt by this?" I tried to fight the tears but found it impossible to do so. "I guess that's the answer. I'm just really hurt."

"It's okay to be hurt, but it isn't okay to be consumed by the hurt. Okay baby, I'm going to run. You should try to get up and moving. Go to the gym, go for a run. I'll see you in a little bit. I love you."

"Love you too babe."

The phone seemed to hang it self up as I sifted Alexander's advice through my mind. I conceded that I needed to crawl out from under the sheets. Because I had a passion for working out, it was a logical way to relieve stress. I told my legs to move, I told my body to crawl out of the bed, but my heart didn't allow either of them to listen. Instead, I decided to lie just a little longer in my misery.

All of the shades were closed, keeping the majority of the winter sun out of the house and allowing me to stumble around the gloomy house in the darkness. I wasn't one to spend the entire day in pajamas. I didn't want Alexander to see just how much of an impact this job situation was having on me. However, before long, the clock read 3:30 p.m. and still not a single light was on. Finally, I dragged my feet to the closet and stood lost in the rows and rows of clothing and shoes that surrounded me. Well over a hundred pair of shoes lined the shelves, neatly ordered by style then color. The clothing followed the same pattern and the quantity bordered on excessive. I always believed in dressing for the career you want and not for the job you have, so I made it a point to put a lot of thought and effort into maintaining a professional look. But again I thought, "What good did that do?"

As I looked at every neat hanger, I became angry. Before long, I found myself tearing through the clothes in a tearful rage. Some ripped; other pieces flew across the room, while a select few simply slid off the hangers as if they were hiding from my wrath. When there were no hanging clothes left in my immediate reach, the shoes got my attention. Heels, pumps, loafers, sandals, peep toes--all tumbled from the shelves in a landslide. Then, silence pierced the anger and caused me to pause just long enough to realize my pain. Sitting on the floor of my closet I was up to my waist in shoes, coats, and clothing. The pity party started again; this was the time to cry it out.

After a few days of adjusting to the news about the position, it was time to formulate a plan. During my battle with depression, I scheduled an appointment for counseling but decided not to go. Instead, I spent time thinking about my next steps. My career goals were simple, and I had already taken the steps educationally to equip myself to attain them. Not getting the director position was harsh proof that I would have to venture in other directions for "opportunities" for growth. I knew deep down in my heart and soul that it was time for a change. Determined to find out where I may have come up short, prompted questions. Was it the interview? Was it my résumé? While I was certain that I had made wonderful networking relationships with my peers, my principals, my supervisors and directors, I took into account that work might still be done in this area.

Getting back into the swing of things was far from easy, and there were mornings that I had to push myself out of bed and into the company of my colleagues. The snubs that came from some mixed with the sympathetic pats on the back from others made facing day after day among my peers unpredictable.

"Okay Relia, you still haven't said much about the whole promotion thing. Girl, if I were you, I'd still be showing out. Everybody knows that Amy wasn't qualified for that job. Who is she anyway? Where did she come from?" stated Anne, my colleague of several years.

"What do you mean? What can I say? We both interviewed, but she was offered the position." I shrugged my shoulders as I spoke, hoping that

I would come across strong and unmoved by my emotions. "I don't know much about Amy."

"Right. That's because she hasn't accomplished anything in the system, at least nothing that I have heard about. Where are the programs she developed? Where are the newspaper articles or the TV coverage? Where is the proof that she has had success in working with our children? Think about it Relia. Nobody knows who she is. How many workshops have you seen her at? How many programs of hers have you heard about? What about presentations? When has she received the Counselor Excellence Award? Have you seen her do any?"

"Nope."

"Exactly. So you tell me how a hearing specialist who just happened to become a counselor but hasn't done anything in this system is all of a sudden qualified to be a director. Honey please. I know better."

"What do you mean?"

"I mean, you have twice as many years and experience as she has. Your track record has been proven time and time again. We all thought you were a perfect fit for that job. Your supervisors and principals hold you in high regards. And all of this would have been fine, if they had chosen someone more qualified or just as qualified as you are. But Relia, she is no where near as qualified as you are. No where close."

I sat quietly and acted as a sounding board. I focused on eating my lunch and tried desperately to appear unmoved by the conversation. I did not care to risk commenting and coming off as bitter. I also didn't want to sound arrogant by agreeing that I was far more qualified than the candidate they chose. However, what Anne was saying only confirmed what I already felt deep down inside was true.

"You know what? I'm sorry. I'm sure that the last thing you want to hear is how you were cheated. It's just that I have a lot of respect for you and the job that you have done here. It's not just that either. Our children need someone who is seriously equipped for the job and understands their needs. And for them to just go and pick up some under-qualified, and might I add, white woman, and give her a job based on nothing, is not only affecting us but most importantly, it's affecting our children." Anne's emotion was beginning to show. She slammed her cup down on the desk and took a moment to try to regain her composure. She breathed deeply, exhaling loudly.

"I really appreciate everything that you're saying. I'd be lying if I said that I wasn't surprised. I was, at first. I don't want to jump to conclusions and assume that Amy was chosen because she was white. I will say this. She must have had a heck of a résumé."

"Or some really good friends. But then again, it is what it is. What can you do? With some things you just have to accept, pray about, and move on." Anne finished up her lunch and exited my office, clearly frustrated by the entire situation.

I went back to eating my lunch, fully engaged in thought. While I'd worked with Anne for some time, she wasn't someone whom I considered a friend or even a close associate. She had nothing to gain in expressing her disappointment to me. There was something about hearing from someone else what I'd been thinking all along that gave me a little bit of peace. Then, the piercing ring of my phone snapped me out of the thoughts. Ever since the embarrassment of not getting the position, I dreaded answering the phone. "This is Dr. Union."

"Dr. Union, this is Nancy, with the Dental Hygiene Program. I'm just touching base with you once again to make sure that we have everything in order for the Dental Program next week. I have everything confirmed here." I sat quietly for a second, trying to recall what this conversation was regarding.

"What time should we come set up?"

"Oh, Nancy. Hello. I am so glad you called. We are anxiously awaiting your arrival. Most of our students have returned their permission forms and are very excited about your visit. As far as setup, we have prepared the perfect classroom as the site. About how much time will you need to prepare?"

"Preparation usually takes a couple of days."

"Okay. We can work Thursday and Friday. The program is scheduled for Monday,Tuesday,and Wednesday at 9:00, so I can get here around 6:45 the first day of the program to let you in so you can put the final touches on the set up."

"Great. You know what? Let's make that 7:30. That should be enough time."

"Are you sure? It's really no problem for me to get here early."

"Yes. I'm positive. Are there any other questions that you have or anything else I can do?"

"No Nancy. You've done more than enough. I'm just so glad that you and your team are going to be able to come and offer this valuable service to all of our students is more than I have imagined." I really appreciated Nancy's genuine tone. "Thanks again Nancy. I'll see you tomorrow."

After speaking with Nancy, my spirits were somewhat lifted. I was excited for my students but still very melancholy. Part of me wondered if someone else in my shoes would have continued to put effort into making this program happen. Why was this type of effort not recognized? I again thought about Amy. My only memories of her in our staff meetings consisted of her unfriendliness. I could have gone on for days with the "whys and why nots", but only a couple of minutes into my thoughts, I had a wake up call. This program was not about me. It wasn't about the administrative staff, or who would get what promotion. It was about the children. They were the reason that I'd given this system more than 20 years and why I came here every day. With my mission refocused and my passion renewed for the moment, my thoughts shifted to making sure that the Dental Program went as smoothly as possible. However, as I worked on tying up a few loose ends for the program, I couldn't help thinking about Anne's statements and wondering if she was right. There were questions that rumbled through my mind. Was there a chance that Amy was awarded a job not based on merit, but on race? If so, was this just another thing that I had to accept? My thoughts carried through the day and leaked into the dinner conversation.

"So what's on your mind?" Alexander was quick to notice how deep I was in thought.

"You want to talk about it?"

"It's nothing really. I've just been thinking about the whole director position thing, and something just isn't sitting right with me about that."

"Why do you say that?"

"Okay. It took me a while to get over the whole thing, but eventually I did. Now it's like every time I turn around I'm hearing the same kind of comments. Who is Amy? Where did she come from? Oh, and my personal favorite, who did she sleep with to get that? Now, I'm not saying that I believe that she slept with somebody to get the job." I jabbered on as Alexander concentrated on finishing his meal. Though he appeared not to be listening, I knew him well enough to know that he was. "I just don't see how she went from being unheard of, to being chosen as a director. It would be one thing if she was an external candidate, but she wasn't. She was internal. As a matter-of-fact, she was a hearing specialist for a while; then she became a counselor, and now she's a director."

"What?" Alexander paused from his meal. "A hearing specialist? Is that considered the same thing as a counselor?"

"No. A counselor works with the entire student body, parents, the faculty, resource people, and administration. We develop programs; we are responsible for parent workshops and meetings; we serve on committees, administer screenings and do any and everything that our principals request of us. We are in our schools the entire day five days a week. On the other hand, she serves a school for a couple of hours a week and only works with one or two students during a session.

"That's a big difference. So has she ever been a teacher? How long has she been a counselor?"

"She has never been a teacher that I know of, and I have twice as many years as she does in counseling. I have never heard her present at any of the workshops or staff meetings. So as a counselor, she flew right under the radar. And I repeat, I do not believe she has any classroom experience. This city, our school system included, is run by African Americans who are in high ranking positions with power to change things. That includes superintendents, directors, supervisors and most of the school board members. In fact, all of Dr. Madeoff's superiors are African American. This should be the one place where discrimination wouldn't be an issue. Surely, they have not forgotten about the great sacrifices made by African Americans for the sake of self-improvement."

"Yeah, you'd think so. But still honey, I can feel it. Something isn't right here." Alexander nodded in agreement.

"Well baby, one thing's for sure. If there's anyone who can figure this thing out, it's you. Just let me know if you need anything from me. I'm behind you 100%, as long as you make me one promise…"

"What's that?"

"…that you will try not to let yourself get hurt." I looked down and went back to eating my meal. While I couldn't see much of a reason that I would end up hurt, I was unable to make that promise. If things were the way they seemed, there would be no getting around the hurt.

Chapter 3 Faces of the Rapists

The brightness of day temporarily blinded her. She blinked quickly, forcing her eyes to adjust. The fog slowly dissipated as she tried desperately to focus on her surroundings. One look at her tattered clothing, and the details of the assault became more and more clear. The room didn't look right. It seemed together and intact, as if no struggle had ever occurred there. There was no sign of her fight, no reason for her or anyone else to believe that an assault had taken place.

The faces of her captors became clear in her mind. Their names flashed in lights above their heads as she tried to make sense of the attack. She knew the "who" but struggled to figure out the "why". Her head pounded painfully, more so from the stress than the physical attack. Her internal wounds far outweighed any external scars. She shook in shame and ducked in defeat, all these feelings secondary to her physical pain.

Just when she gained the courage to move, she heard footsteps. Each step was louder than the last one. For a moment the woman grew optimistic that help was approaching, and then doubt set in. What if the attackers weren't gone? What if they came to finish the job? What if it was a student or a co-worker? She was far too vulnerable to be seen in this state. It's as if the attackers aimed to take one thing but instead left that room with everything: her pride, her confidence, her career, and her joy.

Just as the steps seemed to be closing in on her, she picked herself up. She pulled the tattered edges of her blouse together, trying to maintain at least some of her dignity. Her compact mirror revealed a disheveled appearance and sad eyes. The strength to move on lay deep within her; she struggled to tap into it with every step. Victimized, she pulled her skirt down and quickly tried to put both herself and her classroom back in order. She wasn't done with the situation, but she had to maintain decorum while figuring out her next move. There was a knock on the door. She slowly peeked through the window and saw the distressed face of a student. Battered and bruised, she brushed herself off and opened the door, ready to work with her student.

CHAPTER 3

It didn't take long for me to decide my next move. My thoughts were directed not at what I planned to do, but at how I was going to do it. I felt that it was imperative that I knew exactly what went wrong in my bid for the director position. I knew that things were not as cut and dried as they seemed, and somehow along the way I became more and more assured that it wasn't my qualifications that had kept me from being offered the position. However, it wasn't enough to know it in my heart; I had to prove it to myself and possibly others. Sitting at my desk, thinking about my plan of attack, my thoughts were interrupted by a phone call. "Dr. Union. Can I help you?"

"There is a student here who needs to see you."

"I'll be there shortly." There was nothing unusual about receiving these kinds of phone calls. As a counselor, I had a hand in just about every major incident that occurred in the school. I found it interesting and a little alarming that the phone calls were becoming more and more predictable over the years. In the earlier years of my career, the types of issues that I faced most concerned learning disabilities, ill-behaved students, maybe a few rare abuse cases, and a lack of parental involvement. It seemed that as the times changed, so did the range of major issues that my elementary school aged students were facing on a daily basis. Now issues like parental drug abuse, under-aged sexual activity, molestation, little to no parental involvement, and gangs were rampant among my students. Every time I picked up that phone, I made sure that I was prepared for anything.

"Good morning. Let's walk down to my office. How can I help you?"

"Uhm. I need a bus pass. My teacher told me that I had to get it from you."

"Yes. I can help you with that. What's your name?"

"Carl."

"Carl, what's your last name?"

"Oh. Benson."

"Where do you live?"

"445 Lyndon. You need my apartment number?"

"No, that should be enough. I just need to know what route to set you up for." Administering the bus pass was one of my many routine activities. Because I could do the paperwork for it with my eyes closed, I often found myself bored by the repetition of the paperwork and therefore almost mechanical with the students. However, something about Carl caused me to pause. I looked up from the form that I was writing on and looked at him, something that I tried to remember to do every time I encountered a student. The eyes of a child told his or her story and usually said what could not be spoken. Carl had responsible eyes, yet heavily burdened.

"Okay. Carl, have someone take this letter to the City Bus Transportation Office to pick up your bus pass."

"I thought you were going to give it to me."

"No, I don't give you the actual pass; I just give you the letter that you need to get the pass."

"Well, I don't have a ride to pick it up. That's why I need the pass, because I don't have a ride."

"Isn't there someone who can take you?"

"No Ma'am." I paused somewhat surprised by Carl addressing me as Ma'am. Though I was raised in a time where it was a norm, I found myself facing the daily challenge of teaching my students some of the more basic rules of respect and etiquette. "Okay, how are you getting to school now?"

"However I can. My Mama is sick, and I have to do a lot for her, so she can't bring me. My grandfather used to bring me; now my uncle's girlfriend brings me. Sometimes my teacher or my principal gives me a ride, or I just walk. It just depends..." Carl shrugged his shoulders as if he had nothing more to say about his situation. I took this as a sign that he was not ready to talk about his personal life. I wondered where his father was, how far he traveled to school, and most of whether he was okay. His body language told me that it wasn't the right time to ask, so that was my cue to move on. "Okay how about this?" I suggested after putting my pen down and turning my chair to face Carl directly. "I'll see what I can do to help get the bus pass before this week ends. I can't make any promises, but I'll try." I felt the need to place it on my priority list because of the possible upcoming inclement weather. I could not bear the thought of him walking in the rain, cold, or sleet. Carl nodded but said nothing. "Is that a deal?"

"Yes Ma'am."

"Okay, I'll let your teacher know as soon as I receive it."

"Okay." Carl turned and began to exit quickly.

"Carl."

"Ma'am."

"Feel free to come see me if you need anything else." Carl cracked what looked a lot like a smile, turned, and headed out of my office. Though his request was standard, there was something about him that let me know that his story would be compelling and far from the ordinary. If only he would open up and share with me.

I felt compelled to tell my husband about Carl. It was the first thing I mentioned over dinner. "I met an interesting student today."

"Really."

"Yeah. His name is Carl. I don't know what it is about him Alexander, but I can just tell that this boy is something special. He came to my office for a bus pass, and he was so well-mannered and respectful. He said he didn't have a ride to go pick up the bus pass. Now, don't get me wrong, I've heard that a few times, but something about Carl was different. He appeared more genuine and very sincere. Here he was telling me about the reasons that he couldn't pick it up as if they were only minor setbacks. The information that he shared with me was major, though. He doesn't really have anyone supporting him. His mother is sick, his grandfather used to help out some but doesn't anymore for whatever reason, and his uncle seems to do his own thing. It appears he is truly responsible for himself and even his mother. When I asked him how he got to school, he said he walked when he had to. I looked at his address, and it's not a short walk either. It's at least 45 minutes each way, a long way in the cold or the scorching heat."

"Well, I guess he just does what he has to do. Sometimes life is that way."

"That's the thing. Most children his age haven't really grown into understanding what they have to do. I know with a lot of my students, if Mama isn't there to wake them up in the morning, they don't go to school.

If their ride or the bus doesn't come to their front door and no one tells them to walk, they stay at home. Carl is different though. His mother is sick, and from what I gathered unable to do much for him. But he still does what he has to do to get to school every day."

"And what about you?" Alexander changed the subject very quickly. Seeing my bewilderment, he offered clarification. "Are you willing to do what you have to do?"

"I'm not sure what you mean."

"Well, we both know that you are set on looking deeper into the whole promotion situation. But are you ready for what you may find out? It is one thing to say that you're ready to find out the truth, but it's a completely different thing to say that you're ready to do something about it. I'm just wondering if you've thought this all the way through."

"I haven't really thoroughly reviewed it. I just know that I won't be able to rest easily until I know the facts. That's not to say that I will want to do anything with the truth. For all I know, maybe I lost the position to someone who deserved it more than I did. If that turns out to be the case, then there is nothing I can do but respect it and work harder next time."

"But we both know that isn't the case."

"I hope it is. That would be easier to swallow than knowing that I was passed over for some political reason."

"And what if you were?"

"Were what?" I knew what he was asking me, but I needed to buy myself some more thinking time. I contemplated before simply saying "passed over for political reasons."

"If it turns out that something like that happened, then I'd have to think about my next step."

"I'm only asking this because I know you Relia. You're purpose and principle driven. If this proves to be a situation where you were denied something that was rightfully yours based on something racial or political, you won't stand for it. Your conscience won't let you."

"Yeah. You're probably right."

"And Relia, you could find yourself smack dab in the middle of a fight with half the city. Now I'm here to support you with whatever you choose to do, but I want you to think long and hard about what you could be getting into and what it may take."

Many things really hadn't crossed my mind; I had been so caught up in trying to figure out what had happened, that I hadn't thought about how I'd deal with it once I knew. As I looked over at my husband while he finished his meal, a clear appreciation for his outlook struck me.

His direct approach made me a tad uncomfortable at times, but he is the reason for the balance in this marriage. It works because Relia is the passion, and Alexander is the logic. Of course, there were times when our roles reversed, but for the most part, he's counted on to present the things overlooked by me, the cons versus my pros, or the method to my madness. His unconditional love keeps me in love with him. And even as he finished his meal oblivious to my gaze, he'd unknowingly proved once again to be the insight I needed.

By the following afternoon, after thinking about everything Alexander had said, it was time to continue my quest for the truth, which would drive me to do "whatever it took". The first step was to speak with Dr. Madeoff, the Children's Services Coordinator and a member of my interview panel. She could give me some insight on what happened during my interview process and offer me some constructive criticism, for future reference.

I called and attempted to arrange a meeting with Dr. Madeoff, but was instead referred to Clara Thomas, Supervisor of Social Services. After a few attempts, I was able to schedule a meeting with her. I sat anxiously and watched as she shuffled her papers as if preparing for our conversation. She didn't look up at me until she began to speak.

"Dr. Union, how exactly may I help you?"

"Thank you so much for seeing me. I just wanted to meet with you about the director position that I applied for. I realize that the team has chosen a candidate already; however, I would like to get a better understanding of the criteria used to select the right candidate. When I reviewed the roles, responsibilities, and position requirements, I thought I would be a perfect fit. I have over 20 years experience in a variety of pertinent areas, and my educational background was more than what the job posting required. Is there any insight that you can offer me on this and how the candidates were judged?"

"Well, Dr. Union," answered Clara Thomas looking very uncomfortable as she shifted nervously in her seat. "While certain requirements had to be met, the decision to hire was not based on experience and educational background alone. As a matter of fact, those were the factors that carried the least weight. For this particular position, the decision was made based on the interview. Several counselors applied who were equally experienced and educated. The areas of expertise may have varied somewhat, but for the most part, you were all great candidates with great experience. While your personnel file and record were reviewed and considered, it was the interview that made all the difference. We observed your ability to answer questions under pressure and to articulate your accomplishments within your career. We looked for programming that would be beneficial to our students and in line with the administration's vision."

"Okay..." I paused before saying anything because I was a bit thrown off by her response. I disagreed with the assumption that we were all equally experienced and educated since I have double the years of experience and a higher level of education than Amy, at least. "As far as the interview was concerned, I felt that I did an excellent job in fully answering the questions. I've already demonstrated superior programming and alignment with the administration's vision. I've been nominated for and won awards, awarded grants, and been diligent in continuing my professional development. I've grown up in this system and given far more than the average counselor. So what was I missing?"

"Excuse me?"

"I plan to continue my pursuit in administration, so I would really like to know my strengths and weaknesses. This information will help me to be better prepared in the future."

"I don't think I'm the right person to discuss that with you. You should probably see Dr. Madeoff about that."

"Sure. I would love to speak to her about it as well. After all, she was my supervisor for over five years, and we have known each other professionally for almost 20 years. I was hoping, though, that I could hear it from your point of view as well. That was actually part of the reason I asked to meet with you."

"I wish I could help you, but I can't. You'll have to talk to her about that." Clara Thomas looked at her watch before abruptly wrapping the meeting up. "Is there any thing else I can do for you?"

"I guess not. I'll just try to meet with Dr. Madeoff. Again, thanks for your time."

"You're welcome." I stood to exit the office and noticed that Clara Thomas never looked up to say good-bye, nor did she stand up to see me to the door. I was plagued with uneasiness as I returned to my office. I was certain that she had just fed me a bunch of bull, but I still had no way to prove it. Furthermore, she offered me no constructive criticism for my future endeavors. A meeting with Dr. Madeoff was still in order, and I couldn't let it go.

"Dr. Union?" The voice slightly startled me and snatched me out of my thoughts. The student who needed the bus pass, Carl Benson, handed me a note from his teacher.

"Well, good afternoon Carl."

"My teacher told me to come by your office."

"Yes. I have something for you. Come on in." Carl obediently followed me to my office and had a seat. I reached into my desk drawer and pulled out his bus pass. "I think this belongs to you."

"Thank you." Carl smiled as he took the bus pass out of my hand. He placed the pass in his back pocket and then nervously shoved his hands into his front pockets. He had a beautiful smile that suited his handsome face well. It was contagious and before I knew it, I was smiling too. "You are very welcome. So I guess that means that you won't have to work so hard to get here now?"

"Right. Since my Mama had a stroke she can't do a whole lot for herself. I only miss school when I have to do stuff for her. Some days, she doesn't do so well because of her real bad headaches. We live with my uncle and his girlfriend."

"Oh, well it's good that he's there to help you."

"Not really. It's still just me and my Mama. He's there, but we are kinda in his way."

"Oh. I'm sorry to hear that. Well remember what I said. If there is anything else that you need to talk to me about, feel free to come by."

"All right. Thanks Dr. Union." Questions lingered, and I strongly wished that I could dig a little deeper. I could sense the burden of responsibility that was weighing on him. However, unlike many of the students who were helped, his words were not tinged with resentment and were wise far beyond his years. Watching Carl leave, it became clear that this situation mirrored what Anne had been speaking of that day. Children like Carl needed someone to care not because they were paid to, but because they couldn't help but care. That was the philosophy that kept me working as a counselor. Again, the pain of not getting the position began to ache in my heart. These pains mounted as time passed awaiting the meeting with Dr. Madeoff. I made a mental note to keep in touch with Carl and to try to learn more about his situation, because I wanted to be the support system that he so badly needed.

Because she needed time to review my personnel file, it took several days to get on Dr. Madeoff's calendar. Things had become so unpredictable that nothing surprised me during these follow-up meetings. When I entered her office, she seemed less cordial and even more guarded than she'd been in our previous encounters. I sat awkwardly waiting on her to address me until finally the silence became too much. "Thank you for seeing me Dr. Madeoff. I know the last time that you and I spoke in regards to the director position, you referred me to Ms. Thomas. I did get a chance to meet with her and she informed me that the interview was the major determining factor in choosing a candidate. Because I'm still very interested in a career in administration, I would like to have some feedback on my strengths and weaknesses. I think that knowing this could help me better prepare for a position in administration in the future. She said that she didn't think that she was the right person to discuss that with me and that I should talk to you about that. I totally agreed since you have been my supervisor for the past five years. I would like to hear any feedback that you can offer."

"Well, Dr. Union, I can appreciate you wanting to improve yourself, but I'm afraid I just can't help you."

"Uhm, excuse me." I couldn't believe what I thought I heard her say. "What do you mean you can't help me?"

"I can't help you."

"You were my supervisor for over five years, you, along with Ms. Roberts, nominated me for the counseling award, and we have known each other professionally for almost 20 years. If you can't help me, then tell me who can?"

"Well, Relia. You know what you're good at. You know your strengths. You don't need me to tell you that."

"While I do have my own idea of what my strengths and weaknesses are, I would like to hear it from you." I spoke slowly and calmly as my blood began to boil. "You were on the interview panel. So I would think you have a fresh perspective on what I could do to improve as well as those things that I already do well."

"With all due respect, if you haven't figured out your strengths yet, then what I think should be the least of your worries. Besides, Ms. Thomas has advised me to keep this discussion to a minimum."

I felt my ears get hot, and I found myself inching closer and closer to the edge of my seat, as if in any given moment the levies of my restraint would break and tides and tides of my anger would go crashing towards her. She was crass, condescending, and unwilling to be anything close to helpful. It became clear that this meeting with Dr. Madeoff was not only a waste of my time, but a humbling reminder that my years of faithful service had not earned a single iota of loyalty from her.

In speaking with Alexander about my discussion or lack thereof with Dr.Madeoff, he made some valid points. "Have you checked your record, Relia?"

"No. Why would I?"

"Maybe there's something in your file that made them look past you. I'm not saying that there is, but you do want to make sure that you cover all bases before you start making accusations."

"If I didn't know any better Alexander, I'd think that you don't believe me? What do you mean before I start making accusations? You said yourself that something wasn't right here?"

"Wait a minute. I'm not saying that I don't believe you. And yes, I know that I said something wasn't right. I was there, remember. I do believe you. I know that you were more than deserving of that job. I've been there for the sleepless nights and the tireless hours that you've given that school system; I witnessed the effort that you put into making the dental program and the huge successes of the many other programs. Remember how you involved me and the boys in several of them? I spent months and months in a cold bed while you were away earning that degree. So don't think for one second that I doubt anything that you're saying or feeling. But baby, you have to go about this logically. You have to make sure that you check every single angle on your end before you even begin to look at their end. So far, we know that you met all of the requirements needed, and that you were far more experienced than the selected candidate. What haven't we thought about? What do we not know?" Alexander questioned me again.

"Well, you're right. We don't know what's in my file. However, they are supposed to have me sign any negative report or write-up before it is placed in my file, so there should not be anything there."

"Shouldn't be. But are we sure that there isn't?"

In line with policy, I made an appointment immediately to view my personnel file. I found myself being slightly nervous as I waited on the clerk to come back with my file. While I thought I knew what was in it, there was the slight chance some horrible skeleton, of which I had no knowledge, was hiding in there. The clerk returned quickly with my file.

"Dr. Union, would you please sign and date it here? I'll be right back with your ID."

"Sure." I looked at the inside flap prepared to sign. It was completely empty. "Excuse me. Is a signature and ID required each time it is viewed?"

"Yes."

"Even internally, like administrative staff for promotions, interviews, and so on?"

"Yes Ma'am. A signature is required every single time it is viewed."

"I don't want to seem difficult, but I just want to have a clear understanding of the appropriate procedure. So you're saying that if there are no signatures in a file that it hasn't been pulled at all."

"Correct. Take your file for example. Your signature will be the first signature here, so your file has never been pulled. You are the first person to look at it."

"Okay, thanks." I signed the file quietly. But inside I was screaming. Why was I the first to have looked at my file? Did they not look at it before they selected me to be interviewed? How could they consider me a candidate without checking my personnel file? In our brief meeting, Clara Thomas told me that my file was reviewed and considered lightly, because the interview made the biggest difference. Well, it was now clear that she was being deceitful. No one had ever reviewed my personnel file. When I made my appointment with Dr. Madeoff, I was told that she had to review my file prior to our meeting; that, too, was a lie. My hand shook as I tried to write the date legibly beside my name. I wanted to be certain that my signature appeared at the top with a very legible and indisputable date beside it.

Just as I suspected, my personnel file was strong. It was full of many years of outstanding evaluations. Each of my degrees and certifications were represented and in order. Given the letters of accolade and the exceptional evaluations, my file could easily have been labeled as perfect. I stood with the file in my hand and felt my heart pound in my chest. It was a bittersweet moment. While I was relieved to know that my performance record was just as I thought it would be and absent of any unknown skeletons, I couldn't help but be incredibly disappointed that clearly no one had reviewed it before now. It was like having a badge of honor that couldn't be worn. I always thought that my record would speak for itself when it was time. I now realized that my record was only as good as its exposure; and in this recent process, my record had meant nothing.

"Alexander, you are not going to believe what happened at the record office," I blurted into the phone while leaving the parking lot of the administration building.

"What was in your file?"

"It's not so much about what was in it; it had everything in it that I expected. It's what wasn't in it that I have a problem with."

"Huh?" I could tell he was thoroughly confused. "I don't understand."

"Well, the policy states that a person must show ID and sign a personnel file before reviewing it. This includes for internal reviews, internal hiring processes too."

"Okay."

"When I went to show my ID and sign my file, there weren't any other signatures there."

"Okay…" Alexander still sounded unclear about the point that I was trying to make. "I'm still not real clear about what you're telling me."

"I'm the only one who's ever signed for it. No-one else has ever signed to review my personnel file."

"Oh. So that means that no-one else has pulled it at all."

"That's how it appears."

"Maybe they just didn't sign for it."

"That's what I thought. I asked the clerk, and she was adamant about the fact that everyone shows ID and signs before viewing a file. She said that everyone has to sign. She looked at my file and assured me that no-one else had checked it out because there were no other signatures located any where on my file."

"And she was sure?"

"She was very sure; the evidence was staring us in the face."

"Okay. Well that doesn't seem right."

"You think?" I immediately regretted the sarcasm that oozed from that response. "I'm sorry. I don't mean to get snappy with you. I'm just a little frustrated. I mean, you were right about checking all the bases. Here I was assuming that my file, experience, résumé, and interview weren't enough for me to get the promotion. Now I know that none of that mattered anyway. They didn't know what the full value of my experience was in my file, so my career in this school system wasn't really highlighted. They didn't really get to see the full picture of who I was as a candidate."

"They probably weren't trying to. They would have at least looked at your personnel file if they were really interested in thoroughly screening you."

"Yes. You're right. I guess it's pretty obvious."

"You think?" Alexander said with a light-hearted laugh, returning the sarcastic favor of only moments ago. I couldn't help but laugh with him, as his quick wit was one of his most attractive qualities. "No seriously," he said in an attempt to get back on topic, "What's next?"

"I'm not sure if there is anything left to do."

"I guess it depends on whether you're after peace of mind, or fairness as a principle. If it's peace of mind, then now you have it. You know you did nothing to keep you from getting this job. You didn't stand a chance from the beginning, because more than likely, they already knew who they wanted for it. But if it's fairness as principle that means the most to you, then there is a 'next'. In the pursuit of fairness, the only resolution lies in justice. So I guess that's what you have to think about. What means the most to you right now? Either way, I'd completely respect and understand your decision."

"Yes. I really do have a lot to think about. I'll see you in a bit."

"Ok, baby. Take care and remember. I'll understand and support you either way." I hung up the phone and decided to take a little time to think about the whole situation. My first response was that I was fine now with knowing the truth. I had just needed to know that I wasn't the problem. Seeing my file gave me the answers and reaffirmed my belief in myself. I felt like I could rest easy with that.

The drive from the records office was peaceful. My mind didn't race, my heart didn't pound, and for the first time in weeks, I enjoyed the solitude of being alone. I sighed deeply as I sat down at my desk and attempted to get some productivity out of what remained of my work day. I picked up a recent district newspaper with a post-it note attached to it. It read, "Dr. Union, The Preventive Dental Team would like to thank you for accommodating our Preventive Dental Program in your school. The success of our program relies heavily on people like you. With the help and support of you and your staff, we were able to provide services totaling $118,425.00. Thanks for a remarkable program." I unfolded the paper and was pleasantly surprised to see the article about our Dental Program. There in black and white was a testament of my contribution to not only our school, but to the entire school system. The words that the author of the article used to describe the program were uplifting. When I saw my name in bold letters and the pride that the program brought to our school, memories began to flash through my head. I thought of program after program that I'd instituted during my career, all of which had tremendous impact on my students and the school system. I remembered supporting teachers, counseling students, and mentoring parents. My students were constantly reminded of the importance of education and of being dedicated to the people you are paid to serve, and of how education could shatter glass ceilings and mow down cultural barriers. How could I continue to teach that if I could not continue to believe it? I thought about the years that I had spent working towards the day when I could enhance my knowledge professionally; suddenly, I realized that all of that meant nothing if fairness wasn't a governing principle. How could I continue to work towards being the best that I could be for my students and the teachers who partnered with me everyday, if I didn't feel that my work would be met with integrity and appreciation? I realized right then that my students deserved the best, and until I felt some kind of resolution, my best would be riddled with distraction. Instantly, Alexander's words came to mind and became my cause: "In the pursuit of fairness, the only solution lies in justice. Searching for justice became my next step." I slid the newspaper into my briefcase, cherishing it and the determination it inspired in me. With confidence and just a bit of apprehension I picked up the phone and dialed. "Hello? Is this the EEOC?"

"Yes, how may I direct your call?"

"I would like information on filing a charge."

"So you called them?" Alexander asked that evening. "I thought you were going to think about it."

"I was. But when I got back to my desk, someone had left a copy of the district newspaper article."

"Yeah, I saw that. Congratulations, by the way."

"Thanks. When I read the article, I couldn't help but feel cheated. Yeah, what I do is about the children, but there is a certain amount of attention that the school and the system get from it. Here I am giving everything that I have to this position. The least that I'd like to expect is fairness and the opportunity to grow. It's not so much about me Alexander, it's about my students. I teach them that with hard work and determination, no goal is unattainable. If I don't do my part to make sure that they are treated equally, then my teaching is hypocritical. I just can't stop here. I have to see this thing all the way through."

"Well, it sounds like you're sure about this."

"I can't say that I'm sure; but I have made up my mind."

"You know that there is no turning back after you file that claim right?"

"Yes. I have to give a list of witnesses and a full account of what occurred. They're going to contact every one on the list and give the board time to respond. I suspect that that's when the whirlwind will begin."

"Well, my dear, let the search for justice begin."

My husband and I shared a long gaze of understanding. His support warmed my heart and encouraged my stance. We sat quietly on the sofa and enjoyed the remainder of a movie in peace, each of us silently anticipating the approaching storm.

Chapter 4   Determined to be There for the Children

The eager faces of the students stared back at her. She searched each one, trying desperately to connect to them. Still she felt as if she was being watched. As if just over her shoulder her captors were watching, amused by her discomfort yet in awe of her resilience. Her head pounded and body ached, but still the eager faces of the children tugged at her heart.

Determined to be what they needed first, she continued. Answering their questions, feeding their minds, supporting their growth, and reminding them of their potential, she ignored her own pain. Each time she scowled in pain, she heard their giggles. Yet she continued. Before long, the children provided a welcome distraction from her pain, and it slowly faded into the background.

Soon, the entire assault became nothing more than a vague memory. She wondered if her recollection was failing her. What really happened? Did she cause it? Why didn't any one help her? Perhaps no one helped her because nothing happened. Perhaps no one helped her because she was never really in danger. The day was done, and as the children exited the room excited, the eerie feeling of certain betrayal hung over her. She looked at the phone, unsure of whom to call and what to say. If she reported it, her shame would be revealed for the world to see. She had to be sure. She had to know for certain that her mind wasn't playing tricks on her.

She jumped at a single tap on the door. As if she dreaded whom it would be, she looked slowly over her shoulder. The eyes that peered back at her smiled wickedly and winked before disappearing. They intimidated her. Perhaps they held the key that could unlock her ambiguity. As if her hope rested on it, she ran and threw the door open. There was no one there. She ran up and down the hallway searching desperately. Her legs ached as she moved, each scratch still stinging. Suddenly it all became clear; her doubt cleared, and her suspicions were confirmed. As if revelation lay in the eyes of the missing visitor, she knew what she had to do, and though she dreaded doing it, she knew that she would regret it if she didn't.

She bravely retraced her steps to the scene of the crime. The room, which was still in order, it did not look like the scene of a crime. No signs of a struggle; but still she knew what she had to do. Bravely, she picked up the phone, took a deep breath, and made the call.

CHAPTER 4

By early February, my racial discrimination charges with the EEOC were filed. The process wasn't difficult, but it was rather tedious. However, extra pressure was on me to include more information than they needed. In my opinion, every detail was pertinent, and my reputation for being thorough would be put to the test. They were given my résumé, a copy of the job posting, a list of the people who sat on the interview panels, a list of the people who were not allowed to sit on the panel, and notes from every meeting that I had leading up to the day I filed the claim. I believe that after reviewing all of the information that I submitted, they would have to see what I knew to be true.

It was at a staff meeting that my confidence in my belief was confirmed and maybe even bolstered a little. I sat relatively comfortably amongst my peers and feigned as interest in the discussions. Though the word had begun to spread about the charges that I filed, the faculty and staff remained professional and cordial. "I wonder what she has to say." Faye whispered, as Dr. Madeoff stood up to address the group. "Probably not much," she replied with a sly smile on her face. I ignored her statement, not because I disagreed but because I was, in fact, very interested in what Dr. Madeoff had to say. Ever since my meeting with her, I had wondered how a person could work so closely with me for more than 20 years and yet betray me so easily. Now, I wanted badly for her words to be so redemptive that they would overshadow the betrayal that I felt every time I saw her.

She stood with arrogance and walked up to the podium. Though I gave her my full attention, I didn't hear her first few words; instead, the words from my last meeting with her were ringing in my head, "with all due respect, if you haven't figured your strengths out yet, then what

I think should be the least of your worries." I could still remember her callous expression. It took a conscious effort on my part to snap out of my resentful daydreams and concentrate on what she had to say.

"The findings of the focus group simply reaffirmed what we have already established as target initiatives within the Children's Services Staff. One of the initiatives that the group identified is racial balance. Look around the room. Is it safe to assume that we are racially balanced?" I looked around at the group wondering if anyone else in the room shared my disbelief. I wondered if my ears were playing tricks on me. "Did she just say racial balance?"

"Mm-hmm" Faye rolled her eyes as she answered. "These people know they got a lot of nerve. They will just up and say anything. I don't think I've ever seen anything like it."

"I can't believe that." I rocked anxiously in my seat, determined to get my hands on those initiatives in writing. Something inside of me said that they would definitely come in handy later.

Immediately after the meeting was over, I launched into action. "I was wondering if you will be providing hand-outs, notes, or minutes from today's meeting?" I addressed the young lady who was responsible for keeping the minutes. "I found today's session particularly helpful, and it would be useful to have the notes to refer to later."

"Sure, I just need to organize everything, and then I will make sure that you get a copy."

"I'd really appreciate it."

"It's no problem."

I chuckled a little to myself as I made my way home that evening. As if it wasn't enough that the discrimination was blatantly apparent when it was supposed to be covert, they decided to top things off by making it a key initiative to choose candidates based on race. I couldn't wait to share my new-found information with Alexander.

"So you're telling me that she said that in front of the entire group?"

"Yes!" I answered, as Alexander and I sat on the sofa and enjoyed each other's company. "Racial balance was not on the list for the secondary counselors though. The newly-selected Children's Services Directors for middle and secondary are African American."

"Why not?"

"Well apparently, elementary is the only group that could benefit from having a racially balanced supervisory staff. And I guess three African American Directors would be out of the question."

"Yeah right or maybe…"

"They felt the need…" I couldn't help but finish his sentence. "to justify Amy being hired. I'm sure they know that she wasn't the most qualified candidate. You know, if they know that she wasn't the most qualified, then they would have to know that everyone else knows that she wasn't the most qualified. You know?"

"Yeah I know." Alexander said with a smile. We were both amused at the number of "knows." "It's really good to see you smiling again."

"It feels good."

"It's been months since I've seen you smile like that. I'm sure you still have moments where you're mad as hell or even a little depressed by the whole thing, but I have to admit that you've come a long way."

"Yeah. I have my moments. There are times when I look around at the teachers and how hard they work, day in and day out, with our students, the principals with the almost impossible task of managing the educational needs of hundreds of students, and my peers who must manage the emotional, educational, and social needs of the students, parents, and teachers. I know that I have something to offer and that I could make a difference. Alexander, I have so many ideas. I'm not saying that I have all the answers, but I know this system, and I know what these children need. To be held back by the same people who supported me in the beginning hurts. It kind of cheapens the job and darkens my day. But…"

"I knew there would be a but. You love that job too much for there not to be."

"Yeah. I do. When I meet students like Carl, I get that little ray of sunshine that I need to come back the next day and give it everything I have one more time."

"How is he anyway?"

"Oh he's good. Alexander, he is such a good student. He has even started to open up a little. Every time I see him he has this wonderful smile on his face and these amazingly sincere eyes. I've been getting little bits and pieces of his story here and there. I just learned that his mother had a stroke, which required brain surgery. She is practically unable to care for herself. Remember when I told you that he said his grandfather stopped bringing him to school for whatever reason?"

"Yep."

"Well, his grandfather actually died a while ago. Carl and his mother lived with him up until his death; then they had to go live with his mother's brother."

"His uncle. Well, that's good. At least he has someone to help him with his mother."

"Yeah, he's his uncle, but I don't think it's a good situation. I could be wrong, but I still get the feeling that Carl is carrying way more than a child his age should. Like I said, he's just now becoming comfortable talking more and starting to share certain things with me. So I don't quite have all the details."

"Well, don't push him."

"No. I don't want to add any more pressure to his life. So I just try to make sure that I'm there for him when and if he needs to talk.

"Oh, and what about little Tonya Cole?"

"Can you believe that she's a little gymnast? Mrs. Whitaker actually enrolled her in her daughter's gymnastic classes. Tonya goes home with her every Friday, and Mrs. Whitaker takes them to gymnastic classes on Saturday mornings. And as if that isn't enough, Mrs. Whitaker is paying for everything. Tonya's behavior and grades have improved so much since Mrs. Whitaker took that extra interest in her. It's likes she's finally seen a positive side of life."

It only took me a few days to get the list of initiatives from the staff meeting. I was nearly licking my chops when I saw the term "racial balance" in black and white. In a conversation with Alexander, I decided that it would be beneficial to meet with one of the Associate Superintendents, Dr. Berry. Perhaps she was unaware of how things were being handled and could provide some insight regarding the situation and how it related to me being discriminated against.

I expected to wait several days to get on her calendar, but we actually met within a week of my getting the initiatives in my hand. I guess after months of dealing with all of the different personalities within the administrative system, the usual nervousness that I felt was no longer an issue; I guess you could say that I had a new attitude. With each interaction, I felt my resilience strengthening and my determination growing. I sat in the lobby of the Staff Development Center waiting to be called into her office. I stared at the sheet of paper, ensuring that the intent of it hadn't changed. I was anxious to hear her response, but wanted to be sure that I presented it in the right way. The last thing I wanted was to come across as confrontational.

Dr. Berry approached me, moving very quickly with a notepad under her arm. I stood and gathered my things, prepared to follow her back into her office. Berry shook my hand as she greeted me. "Good afternoon Dr. Union."

"Good after-," before I could finish the statement, she sat down in one of the seats directly across from me in the lobby. I was careful not to allow my face to reveal how shocked I was by the fact that she obviously wanted to have this discussion in the lobby. I expected to be able to share my concerns within the privacy of her office. Never did I expect her to be so flippant about what I had to say, or unprofessional in her approach. It was as if I was not welcome in her space, and she had no intention of spending a long time with me. But just as I adjusted to all of the other crap, I adjusted to this and had a seat. "So, how can I help you?"

"I'm not sure whether anyone has brought this to your attention, but I have a few concerns about the hiring process for one of your recent job postings. I feel that I may have been overlooked for a position not based on merit but based on my race." I studied her expression as I spoke, waiting for a clue as to her impression of the situation. I was unsure of how much she knew, what she'd been told, or how she felt about the whole thing. Her expression did not change. She maintained a poker face and sat straight up, cold and professional. "I have a couple of questions and would love to hear your professional opinion on everything."

"Okay."

"Well," I was unsure of where to start. Her very matter-of-fact tone was slightly intimidating. "I've been in the school system for more than 20 years. I've worked my way from a substitute teacher to a classroom teacher to a counselor. I have served as acting principal and acting director. My time has also been spent as an adjunct professor. My educational background includes certification in administration and supervision and a doctorate in curriculum, instruction and policy study. I am certified as a licensed counselor by our state board. Therefore, I decided that it was time for me to pursue opportunities for growth and to serve our students in a different capacity. This is how my interest in the Children's Services Director came up. When I applied for the director position, I expected the position to be filled based on the criteria outlined in the job posting as well as the overall qualifications of each applicant. To my knowledge, the applicant who was selected did not have the experience specified in the posting. Her résumé wasn't nearly as impressive as mine or those of some of the other applicants. So it seems that she was chosen based on something other than qualifications. In our staff meeting, Dr. Madeoff outlined some key initiatives for the elementary group. One of those was racial balance."

"Yes, that's correct."

"My concern is that Amy Folder was selected for the position to help attain racial balance. She was the only white candidate. I truly feel that is the reason that I wasn't fairly considered for the position. To be looked over for a promotion because of my race is morally wrong; however, to have an unqualified candidate chosen strictly because of race is detrimental not only to the morale of the staff but even more so to our students."

"Dr. Union, you've made some very valid points today. Yes, we do have to attain and maintain racial balance. Diversity is very important to not only the elementary group, but also to the school system as a whole. We want each and every student fairly represented, and the key to doing that is by working towards having a balanced teaching and administrative staff. That being said, Dr. Madeoff should have selected a more qualified pool of whites. The key is to get the best possible candidate while maintaining that balance." There it was. She said it. Amy Folder was not the most qualified candidate. She was chosen to maintain racial balance, with no consideration given to her lack of qualifications and inexperience. If only the EEOC could have been a fly on the wall.

Dr. Berry seemed comfortable as she continued to speak. "I depend on the people whom I put in charge to do the right thing. I was overlooked once. The position was given to a white male, but I continued to work hard for our children. It took a minute, but eventually my potential was seen, and my work was rewarded. So I do know how it feels to be overlooked."

There was an awkward silence as Berry sat and considered how to convince me. I didn't know what to make of her. She came across as trustworthy, but I was unsure of just how valid her statements really were. I wanted to trust her, but past experiences made it impossible to do so. Berry finally broke the silence in an attempt to smooth things out.

"Here's what I'll do. I am going to look into this a little further. I'll speak to both Dr. Madeoff and Mrs. Thomas about this and get back to you."

"I would really appreciate it. I still plan to pursue a position in administration in the future. Any help that you could offer to prevent this type of thing from happening again would be appreciated."

"Sure. Just let me talk to them, and I will get back with you. Again, thank you for bringing this to my attention."

"Thanks for seeing me." Dr. Berry stood up and walked back to her office. She had not taken a single note. She didn't write down my concerns or even speak as if she was familiar with me as a long time contributor to this school system. Instead she walked away, certain that she'd done just enough to placate me.

During the drive home, I reflected on the awkward meeting and became even more frustrated that Alexander would have to hear that nothing would be done to correct the problem.

"Wait baby, I don't want you jumping to conclusions. Maybe she does intend to look into it. I don't want you to get so caught up in your experiences with the other people. Give her a chance."

"I don't know Alexander. I can't help but feel like she has a little to do with this whole thing. She sounded sincere, but I'm not sure I believe any of it. It's easy to shift the blame on your people, especially when the people you're blaming aren't there to speak up or defend themselves. I'd be willing to bet that her people were working with her approval."

"That may be true, but until you're sure, you have to take things at face value."

"So what's next?"

"Relia, thank the woman for her time. See if she gets back to you. If she does, listen to what she has to say. If she doesn't, then at least you know where she fits in the puzzle."

"Well, I've already sent her a follow-up letter thanking her for her time. I did that right after the meeting. All I can do now is wait to see what she does next. Hopefully, she'll prove me wrong."

"Yeah, hopefully she will."

"But I doubt it."

"Relia Union, you are one stubborn lady."

"I just call it like I see it. Like I said, I hope that she proves me wrong." Alexander laughed at my stubbornness as he eyed me lovingly.

Though I was pretty sure that a response shouldn't have taken that long, a month passed, and I still hadn't heard anything back from Dr. Berry. I made several phone calls, left messages, and e-mails, but none were returned. Concerned that she hadn't responded, nonetheless, I stayed so busy with my Career Awareness and Tutoring Program that it all hadn't had a chance to sink in. With just over a month and a half left in the school year, we were getting to a crucial point in our basic skills training portal. This program proved to be a great success: I was visited by our local

TV reporter, and imagine my excitement when I learned that our Career Awareness and Tutoring Program made the five o'clock news.

In this program, I worked towards two objectives: One was helping students see the relationship between school and career; the other was providing tutoring to those students who were having trouble with their basic skills. However, we were approaching the testing season, and the tutoring component of the program had to be accelerated in preparation for our end of the year standardized testing. In working on this, I became so focused on my students that weeks flew by before it hit me that Dr. Berry had not only failed to contact me, but she hadn't returned any of my phone calls or e-mail. After about five weeks of waiting, I gave up and accepted the fact that she too was unable to maintain professionalism or take accountability for what were obviously blatantly discriminatory practices. Mentally, I made a check by her name and waited to hear from the EEOC.

My days at school seemed to get longer and longer as the end of the school year approached. I found myself putting in hours and hours of work preparing our students for the next step in their growth and development. I maintained an open door policy for the students, the faculty, and even the staff. One afternoon, long after the students had left for the day, one of our dedicated school volunteer, Mr. Mason, entered my office. Mr. Mason lived in the neighborhood, and had been a volunteer 15 plus years. He provided little informational tips, acting like a community liaison who knows the history of our students. I could always count on him to give me any needed help with our students and to do whatever was necessary to help with our school projects.

"Dr. Union?"

"Hey, Mr. Mason. Come on in. What can I help you with?"

"Well, I know that you have a way of getting funding for things. It's been said that if anyone has questions about grants or funding, that you are the one to talk to."

"I don't know about all that. But I'll try to bring in as many resources as I can. What are you looking to do?"

"You know that we have the basketball program for the students."

"Yes."

"I have some good kids on the team. They're all excited about the season, but there's just one problem. I don't have the money to do it. We've got a few balls for them to practice with, but we don't have uniforms, water bottles, etc. The team isn't counted in the budget, so we don't have access to money like some of the other programs here. Everything we do is based on donations and what I call creative funding. So I was thinking, maybe you could help me get one of those grants that you use to pull off all those programs that you been putting on." I scanned my mind for any funding that I could remember hearing about that he could use. Nothing came to me right offhand.

"Dr. Union, I know it's a long shot. I just want my kids to be able to play. It's too important to them."

"I'm sure it is. I think it's great that you care so much, and I want to help you. I'm just not sure how I can yet. When would you need the uniforms?"

"The season doesn't start for a few months."

"The whole grant process can take months. I can't say for certain that we could write and be awarded a grant before your deadline. Sometimes those things move faster than others, but I just can't guarantee it."

"Oh, I understand." Mr. Mason looked disheartened. "I would have started earlier, but we just really got the team going."

"Wait, let's not give up so fast. I'm going to check on a few options and see what other alternatives we have. How many players do you have?"

"Ten."

"Okay. Give me a few days to see what I can find out."

"I'd sure appreciate the help."

"Don't thank me yet; if we're lucky, you can thank me later."

"Let's hope so. I don't want to hold you any longer. You should have been gone a long time ago."

"I tend to work longer hours at the end of the year. But I'm on my way out now. I'll actually be right behind you. You have a wonderful evening." Mr. Mason made an exit while I gathered my things. I was pretty sure that I wouldn't be able to find that type of funding; needing it that quickly would make it even less likely. I was certain of one thing, however. I would not let something as simple as uniforms stop the students from participating. For most of them, this would be their only chance to be involved in any extracurricular activity. In the majority of the cases, our parents are unable to provide transportation for our students. Therefore, they are usually unaware of all the wonderful options outside of their neighborhood.

After searching for a few days, I was still unable to locate a grant or any other source of funding for Mr. Mason's basketball team. "Well Mr.

Mason, I think I told you that it would be difficult to find that type of grant. I have to be honest with you. I haven't been able to find one yet."

"I understand. Thanks for trying though."

"I talked to a few people, though. Maybe we can get some kind of local business to sponsor the team. They could pay for the uniforms as a part of the sponsorship. My husband's company may be interested." I tried not to let on, but I had already talked to Alexander about it, and he was willing to sponsor the team. "Maybe I could arrange for you to talk to him about purchasing the uniforms."

"Sure, if it wouldn't be too much to ask. I'd love to talk to him about it. I'll do whatever it takes to make sure that I don't let those kids down."

Just then, my principal, Mr. Williams, walked in. "Good afternoon Dr. Union. Can I speak with you for a moment?"

"Sure."

"There really isn't an easy way to say this, so I'll just get right to the point. We're in a budgeting crunch for next year, and we've had to look at some ways to balance our deficit. I'm afraid that your position has been declared surplus. You can always look for other positions in the system, though. Of course, I'd be more than willing to give you a great letter of reference."

"Wait a second. I don't understand. How was I declared surplus? I was present at our last School Council meeting and there was no mention of any counselors being cut from the budget. I still have the minutes."

"Dr. Union," Mr. Mason cut in, clearly uncomfortable with where the conversation was going. I found it to be completely unprofessional of Mr. Williams to say this in front of Mr. Mason.

"I appreciate the help. We can just talk about the uniforms tomorrow." stated Mr. Mason.

"Oh," Mr. Williams stuttered. "I didn't realize that you were still in a meeting. We can talk about this at another time." He'd been so focused on what he had to say to me that he missed the fact that we weren't alone in the room. Though I was more interested in finishing the conversation about my job, I didn't want to do it in front of Mr. Mason. "I'm actually just finishing up with Mr. Mason. There's no need to leave." I wrote Alexander's number down on a post-it note. When I looked up to hand the note to Mr. Mason, Mr. Williams was gone.

"Here's the number at his office. Just give him a call tomorrow. I'm sure you can work something out."

"Thanks again. I really appreciate the help." Mr. Mason started to exit but paused thoughtfully. "Look, I don't mean to speak out of turn, but I just gotta say this. I would have run out of here too if I were him. He knows that you're just about the best thing going at this school. It would be a shame to lose you. I'm just not a big fan of the politics that they play around here. This job shouldn't be about the politics; it should be about the kids. At the end of the day, they are the ones who count, and if we don't get it right, they are the ones who'll suffer."

"I appreciate it. What I do is just a small part of the whole piece. You, the teachers, and the rest of the staff are always working hard to help each and every child. So while it's nice to have your support, I'm more concerned about how I can support all of you. I will say this though-- I'm here for our children, and I'll fight for them. So surplus or not, don't count me out yet." Mr. Mason smiled and continued to the door. He looked back over his shoulder. "Now that's what I want to hear."

I was certain that Mr. Williams passed Mr. Mason in the hallway because he walked back in only moments after Mr. Mason's exit. I immediately started in on him. "Like I was saying, I attended the School Council meeting and nothing was said about counselors being cut from the budget. It was clearly stated that we would discuss the budget in the next meeting. The next meeting never materialized, so how did you manage to come to the conclusion that I'm surplus?"

"Yes, you're right. We didn't get a chance to talk about this in the School Council meeting. This kind of came out of nowhere, and I was just looking for options."

"Out of nowhere, huh?"

"Yes, but I apologize. It was my mistake, and I didn't mean to alarm you. You can stay. We'll just have to look in other directions to make up the difference."

The rest of Mr. Williams' pathetic speech went in one ear and out the other. By now it was no big secret that I'd filed charges with the EEOC. I was certain that for the school system, the games had begun, and I was no longer just an employee; I was a problem.

"So are you surprised?" Alexander asked as I spoke with him on my way home. "Didn't we expect them to do something to try to get back at you?"

"Yeah, but I don't think I expected it to be so out in the open. They didn't even make an effort to make it seem like something other than retaliation. They had to know that it would be obvious to approach me about me being surplus."

"Why? Everything else has been obvious. Why wouldn't this be?"

"Well, even if there was a budget issue, which I know there isn't, he is still out of order. I made a phone call to the board, and I was told there was no budget issue regarding counselors. He knows how long and dedicated I have been to that school. He didn't even give me my option to stay in a teaching position. One of the main purposes of the School Council is to make decisions as a team about the budget and any other matter concerning the school. He is not supposed to make a decision without consulting with the entire Council. That's not how it works."

"I guess when you have the clout that they obviously think they have, things work however you want them to."

"Well, not if I have anything to do with it."

"Somehow baby, that just doesn't surprise me."

Things were relatively quiet for the rest of the school year. Despite the political issues, we ended our school year on a high note. The mentoring program increased parental involvement and decreased student behavior issues. Our end of the year standardized test scores improved moderately, and the basketball team got uniforms through Alexander's sponsorship. I was only a month into summer break when I received the Dismissal and Notice of Rights to Sue. My immediate response was to request a meeting between myself, the system, and the EEOC. Just as I expected, the system was unwilling to meet and stood firm on their claim of no wrongdoing. The EEOC stated that they were unable to find any evidence of racial discrimination and in line with their legal obligations, sent me the documentation relating to my claim.

The packet from the EEOC also held the paperwork that the EEOC had received from the board. Their documentation included the following: Amy Folder's résumé; the participants; panel members; computer generated scores of each interview; and blank forms, but no raw data.

"Okay, let's look at this. I have to try to understand how they could have missed the apparent evidence of discrimination. I have to see what they saw."

"I doubt that everything is here."

"I'm sure you're right." I began to go through each piece with a fine-tooth comb. The discrepancies quickly piled up and before long the EEOC's lack of due process was unmistakable.

"No wonder they found no evidence. They didn't look for any." I took the pile of documents and pointed a few of the issues out to Alexander. "Okay, here is a list of the board policies. I've highlighted some of the glaring errors. I haven't made it through the packet, but as you can see, there are discrepancies. And look. These are supposed to be the scores from the interview, but they aren't the raw scores. This is a summary of the composite scores, but it doesn't show what each interviewer actually wrote. How do we know that these composites are correct? We don't. I am sure they listed information that would support their statements. Not to mention the fact that Amy's résumé is so ambiguous, she is clearly not qualified for the position. There is no degree listed by counseling and guidance. Does she have a Masters, Ed.D., Ph.D.?"

"That figures."

"I know. Several people are in administrative positions who are not truly qualified. Let's take Dr. Madeoff, for example. She does not hold a certification in elementary counseling. She's never had any experience with our young developing children whether it was in counseling or the classroom. She was strictly high school. This may explain why in five years of being under her supervision, neither I nor any of the elementary counselors that I know has ever received a supervisory visit from her. Our friend, Clara Thomas, is not certified in administration. And based on Amy's résumé, there is no degree listed for counseling. But what do they do? They give her an administrative position."

"Yeah," my husband replied sarcastically. "That makes sense. What about the witnesses you listed? Didn't they help any?"

"Unless something has changed in the last week, none of them was ever contacted by the EEOC or school system to give a statement."

"Wow. So it looks like the EEOC really had no intention of giving this charge a good hard look. I was told by an attorney that because the school system is a government agency, the EEOC would turn their heads to any wrong-doing. I even noticed that they had adopted a school. There was a plaque on their wall stating that they were the adopters of a school for five years. I guess the average citizen just doesn't have a fighting chance."

"That's what it looks like."

"Well, look who they're researching. This is the school system. I don't think too many organizations, private or government owned, would want to go up against them."

"Yeah you're probably right. I'm going to think on this some. I'm already all in; I'm not sure if I can just stop now. I am being targeted, and the way I see it, it'll only get worse."

"Yeah, you're probably right."

Alexander watched as I sat on the floor and studied each document from EEOC. Armed with my date book, my highlighter, a calendar, board policies, and my own documentation, I continued to break down the lies in each document.

"Well, baby", Alexander spoke in a calming and reassuring manner. "The good news is you are the perfect person to look through this. You're sharp, and if anyone can smell a rat, it's you. Look over the documentation and take as much time as you need to process it all. You have the rest of the summer left to work on it, and you still have time to file a lawsuit, if you decide to."

"No, I really don't. Don't you get it? They have already started the retaliation. The whole surplus thing is only the tip of the iceberg. Those people are going to try to make my life a living hell. Now, I love my students and I love my job, so I don't plan on giving up without a fight. But as is always the case with fights, somebody is bound to lose."

Chapter 5   The Police Station

"Okay, if you'll just have a seat, an officer will be with you shortly." She obediently took a seat and looked around at the activity going on in the police station that day. The place was full of riftraft and troublemakers, all with their own stories to tell. What, she thought, would make her story any different?

The report was long and tedious. She sighed as she looked ahead at the long list of questions that she had to answer. She dreaded it and went back and forth between regretting her decision to report it and wanting to make sure that it never happened to anyone else. Fear and selfishness distracted her from justice and righteousness, making it hard for her to go on. She ploughed on and completed the report as clearly and accurately as she possibly could.

She hoped her eyes would tell the story, that her hurt would be interpreted and seen as proof that she had, in fact been raped. She hoped that the physical examination would offer conclusive evidence that she was different from the other miscreants who came in with their dog and pony shows.

"So, I see here that you were familiar with your attackers?"

"Yes. I was."

"How familiar?"

"I have worked with them for several years now."

"Okay-." The officer replied sarcastically as he made notes on her report. She knew that doubt had already begun to form in his mind. "And are you willing to have a physical examination for the purpose of gathering evidence?"

"Yes, of course."

"Okay. I think that's about all I need right now. An investigator will contact you shortly." The officer closed *her file and walked away. She was reluctant to leave, sure that there was something more that needed to be done. She was certain that a physical exam was supposed to be done immediately. "Excuse me," she spoke quietly yet firmly, in an attempt to get the officer's attention. "What about the examination?"*

"What about it?"

"Isn't that supposed to be done immediately? You know like, before I take a bath, while the evidence is still there."

"I suppose so. Wait here; I'll find someone who can help you with that." The officer was gone for about 20 minutes before a female officer returned and picked up the clipboard holding the report. The officer walked up the hallway and yelled over her shoulder, "Come with me." The nervous woman followed the officer into a room that had nothing but a table and bare white walls. The officer dropped the clipboard on the table causing a loud crash that startled the fearful accuser. The officer stood facing her with her arms crossed. She stared as if there were hundreds of places she would rather have been.

"So?", the office stated.

"Uhmm," the woman replied, unsure of what to say next, "so?"

"So, are you gonna take off your clothes? Today?" The officer spewed sarcasm much to the bewilderment of the victim. She obediently undressed, making sure she avoided eye contact with the officer.

"Turn and face that wall and hold your arms straight out." Chills went down the woman's spine as she cringed from the discomfort of being examined like side show cattle. "Now turn and face me." Same discomfort, same goose bumps. "Spread your legs and bend over."

"Is this really necessary?"

"I'm just looking for visible signs of trauma. You know like bruising, cuts, scratches, or anything that will show signs of a physical altercation. I'm also looking for any DNA evidence that may have been left behind."

"Oh. Okay."

"Here is something. I'm gonna take a picture, for evidence."

"Okay." The small sound of the flash startled the shaken woman again. The officer picked up the clipboard. *"Okay, I think that's about all that I need."*

"What about...?"

"The inside? If you let me finish, I'll tell you about that too. What I was about to say is that you need to go to the hospital now. You can go in the emergency room of that hospital right up the street. We can call and let them know to expect you so that you don't have to wait so long. They will do another external examination, take more pictures, and look at..."

"...The inside?"

"Yes, the inside. They will be able to tell if there are signs of forced intercourse, and any other key indicators that usually exist when a person has been raped. I've been told that it isn't the most pleasant experience, especially after going through something like a rape. But if you are serious about reporting this and possibly prosecuting your attackers, you really do need to go and get examined."

There was an awkward silence for a minute as the officer made her way to the door. *"I need to get this put in the computer. The report will be on file and available for pickup in seven to ten days. If you have any questions in the meantime, or if you remember any additional details, please give me a call."* The officer handed the still naked woman a card. *"Take your time getting dressed. I'll call the hospital and let them know to expect you."*

Sometime between getting dressed and exiting the examination room, the officer seemed to soften up. Though she was unsure of what had caused the hostility in the first place, the woman couldn't help but feel less victimized once it had subsided.

CHAPTER 5

The more that we discussed the EEOC findings, the more certain we became about the need for justice, so we began an intensive search for an attorney. After meeting and talking with the first 30 attorneys, it was painfully clear that no one wanted to go to war with the school system. Those few who seemed willing were not confident about the strength of my case. The routine became familiar. They would look over the paperwork, then look up at me, look back down at the paperwork, then look at me. Then, they would give their temple a nervous rub, take off their glasses if they had them, and sigh. When they finally found the words to speak, they would usually start by saying, "Look, I really appreciate you meeting with us today, and can appreciate your need to pursue something like this, but..." What came after the "but" varied, but the end results were the same. Over and over again, I was denied, and told that I had no case.

For many of the attorneys, it was simply a conflict of interest. The school system is a business associate and a major contributor to many important firms. It emerged that they have a hand in everything. One attorney told me that he'd think about it and give me a call. Needless to say, that call never came, and it took weeks of me calling him to figure out that he wouldn't be contacting me. I met with lawyers of all races, both genders, and several different religions. My search included costly, well-established attorneys and rookies who had nothing to lose.

"Are they even taking the time to review the information before they turn the case down?" asked Alexander.

"Yes. I think they are. Well, let me put it this way. They pretend to listen to my story, act like they're reviewing the paperwork, and then they say they can't help me." I don't believe any one has the guts to take on my case."

"But why?" Alexander seemed even more perplexed than me.

"I mean, anybody can look at that stack of paperwork the EEOC sent you and tell that something isn't right."

"Well, I'd like to think so. I know it's evident to me, but then again I lived it."

"Look at this résumé." Alexander picked up Amy Folder's résumé and held it up. "It's ridiculous. It doesn't even spell out whether or not she has a Bachelor or a Masters degree."

"That's if she has one at all. This situation has been so confusing."

"We only have another month or so to file this lawsuit. We need to turn the heat up on our search."

"Well," I replied hesitantly. "I could represent myself."

"Baby, this is federal law. Don't get me wrong. You're sharp. But federal law is a whole different ball game. That would be too much for you to take on. Just be patient; somebody will come along. Trust me. Things will work out just the way that they're meant to."

"I guess you're right. But still, if we don't find someone, I'm ready to do what I have to do."

"From you Relia baby, I wouldn't expect anything less." Alexander answered with a smirk as he lovingly made fun of my tendency to be overly prepared and somewhat overzealous in everything I did.

The search for an attorney consumed my whole existence during the break from school. I spent the entire summer scanning the EEOC documents, researching precedents, meeting with lawyers, and preparing to represent myself just in case. School would be starting again in only a couple of weeks, and I felt like I'd yet to make any real progress. Only a few teachers roamed the hall, and I enjoyed the peace and quiet that the beginning of the year would bring. I decided to take advantage of it and get a head start on developing my programs, working on my schedules for classroom guidance sessions and contacting my resource people. I finally got the number for the surgeon who would make the perfect mentor for one of my special cases, John Pitts. He was unavailable, so I left him a vague message that didn't give him all the details about John. John was a survivor by all accounts. In just a few short years, he'd gone through more than many adults. His mother had a tragic addiction to crack, and her craving for the poison had gotten so strong that John became her personal barter object. For years, he was traded for drugs, and used as a sexual toy by any dealer who would stoop that low. This tragic life had affected John in a way that made him a behavioral issue for his special education teacher and her assistants. And he had become his own worst enemy. I knew that we had to do something drastic to get him on track and to give him at least a shot at life. We decided the most difficult time for him, his five other emotionally disturbed classmates, and his teachers was after lunch, so we scheduled a bus to pick him up after lunch and deliver him to his front door. This solved the disruption problem. However, he still needed more. I decided that a mentor would be a crucial part of John's restoration. A mentor, perhaps, could give John a peek into what the world can be like outside of the mean streets of the hood. This surgeon could help John see that hard work could uplift him from what appeared to be a grim situation.

The end of the summer routine was normal, the smell of nostalgic, and I often felt a little twinge of excitement when I saw the janitors giving the floor that new school year shine. They always took such pride in making the school look its best. They were in a loud, deep discussion outside my office where they were prepping the floor. I listened closely.

"That's why I'm glad that we have that whole union thing," said one janitor. I have a feeling they will take care of us."

"Yeah. I guess. I don't see what the big deal is though. Do you really think we can beat this whole dang system? We're talking about the school system here. The city school system; you can't get any bigger than that here in this city."

"Yeah, but I'm still going to that meeting!" the janitor repeated with excitement.

"What meeting?"

"The union has some attorneys meeting with all of us tonight. They are supposed to talk to us about our case."

Rumblings of this meeting had circulated but didn't register with me until the janitors spoke of it. Something hit me when they said the word "case", and without much of a second thought, I found myself traveling some two hours to the neighboring state to their meeting hoping to meet the attorney who could possibly represent me.

Had I taken too long to think about it, I probably would have decided against traveling in a thunderstorm at night to a small town that I knew absolutely nothing about. The rain battered against my umbrella in loud, hard drops as I shuffled across the parking lot of a small church. When the door slammed behind me, every head in the room turned and looked at me. I was obviously out of place among janitors and some maintenance workers, most of whom were still dressed in their work clothes. I walked in poised and together as if I was certain that I was in the correct place. It took almost three hours for the attorney, Joseph Grassley, to finish his meeting with the janitors and take a few minutes to speak with me. After giving him a quick run-down of my case, he took my number and promised to give me a call after he had had a chance to look a few things over.

Unexpectedly, Attorney Grassley called back the next day.

"Dr. Union, this is quite a case you have here," he said in a tone that was encouraging yet disappointing. "You definitely have a fight on your hands, but I think you have a pretty good chance."

"Great!" It was like a weight had lifted off my shoulders.

"So what's next?"

"What I was going to say is, though I really believe you have a solid case, and I'm not sure that we are the right firm to handle it."

"Oh," with greater force than before, the weight collapsed right back down on my chest as disappointment set in. "Why? What's the problem?"

"Well, I can't commit to taking on the case right now. I just don't know enough about it. We don't know what judge you'll be getting; we don't know much about the candidate who got the job; and, we don't know much about the other candidates who may have been overlooked. Those details are crucial, and right now we are just too uninformed to make any major commitments. Unfortunately, time isn't a luxury that we have right now. Although we don't have enough time to do the proper research that a case like this calls for, I would like to try to help you."

"Okay. I'd appreciate all the help I can get right now."

"The deadline is closely approaching, correct?"

"Yes, only a few weeks left."

"I can write the complaint for you, and you can file it yourself. They have 30 days to show and prove. If they don't respond, you win; and if they do respond, you'll know what they're working with. Let's see what happens and then we can revisit things."

"Okay..." My response was slow as I tried to grasp some kind of understanding of what this would mean to my case and whether it would put me at a disadvantage. "So what would that cost me?"

"In the formal consultation, we can look at an hourly rate and the processing fee. Believe me, I'm passionate about this kind of thing, and

I want to make sure that we give you the best possible deal. The thing that's most important to me is that you have the opportunity to file your paperwork in time. We can look at your options from there."

"Okay, that sounds reasonable, but I really need to talk this over with my husband. Is it okay if I give you a call a little later and let you know something?"

"Sure. If you can't get me, just talk to my receptionist."

"Okay, I'll give you a call. Take care."

"You too, Dr. Union."

When I hung up with Attorney Grassley, I couldn't help but feel that for the first time since this case had started, I was making real progress. I was unsure of where it would take me, but for once it felt like I was going somewhere.

Though the hustle and bustle of finding an attorney kept me running and my mind occupied, I always found myself excited about the idea of seeing the smiling faces of my students. Our new students provided a clean slate and another opportunity to affect change, while my repeating students were like my very own children. There was always some concern for my children who were advancing to the next level. I struggled with this because they just weren't prepared, and that we may have sent them blindly to a less understanding world. Though it was a bit unsettling, I tried to focus on the students who were currently under my care and take every opportunity to give them an outstanding learning experience. Most of them were considered at risk. This meant that they were not going to have the skills or education that they would need to be successful in society. Therefore, I made it my main goal to do everything that I could to help prepare them to be successful in today's society.

I sat and compared some of the changes in my curriculum as the hallways buzzed with new students.

"Hey, Doctor Union."

"Hey, there Carl. How was your summer?"

"It was okay. I'm gonna need another bus pass."

"Okay." I took out the form and began to fill it out for him. "So how's your Mom?"

"Okay."

"And your uncle?"

"Don't know. I haven't really heard from him since we moved." I paused from writing and looked up at Carl. "You moved? Where are you staying now?"

"Somebody helped us out and gave us a place. We're staying there until we can find a place of our own." I listened to Carl, amazed at how composed and grown-up he sounded. Again, I recognized the need to refrain from pushing the subject. I found that Carl had a way of sharing his feelings in parts and slowly letting me into his world. He sat in silence as I finished up the last few lines of the form. "I'll get this to the City Bus Transportation Office and call you when it is ready."

"Thanks a lot. I gotta go. My teacher told me to come straight back."

"Okay. Carl, it was good to see you."

I smiled until Carl was long gone. His spirit was encouraging to me and gave me a sense of hope. I took Carl's bus pass form and tucked it into my day planner, so that I'd remember to pick his pass up for him.

Minutes later, Miss Duckett, my co-counselor popped her head into my room. "Dr. Union? Do you have a minute?"

"Sure, come on in."

"I'll only take a couple of minutes. Mr. Williams wanted me to look over your list of targeted at-risk students." Her direct approach surprised me. She took a deep breath before continuing, "You know, just to make sure that we're all on the same page."

"What do you mean look over it? He usually looks over it with me. We meet at the beginning of every year and discuss it."

"I know, but this year, he asked me to look over yours and just report back to him.

"I just think that he should have informed me, that's all." I slowly looked through my files and pulled my list out. As Miss Duckett and I compared notes, I couldn't help but wonder if this was just the beginning of a wall of separation that Mr. Williams was building between us.

I still remembered the first time that I ever met with Mr. Williams. He was kind and seemed very dependent on me and my opinion. He had the potential to be flirty, but my professionalism kept him on track. Before long, I had become his "wing man." Over the years, Mr. Williams had been given numerous awards stemming from my projects. Our school had been represented in the newspaper time after time for accomplishments that were a result of my hard work and dedication as well as his trust in my abilities. That said, the thought of him alienating me was more shocking than hurtful. I carried this feeling with me through the remainder of the school day.

The day moved on and soon thoughts about the drive home and dinner came. As always, I monopolized the dinner conversation with my thoughts and worries. Alexander listened carefully but said nothing. His expression was one of reserve. I paused, hoping that he would chime in. He said nothing. I talked a little more and paused again. "Okay Alexander, am I talking to myself?"

"Nope, I'm just listening."

"You look like you want to say something."

"Not really. I'm just listening."

"So?" I prodded, trying to get some type of reaction. "What do you think?"

"About what?"

"About Mr. Williams telling Miss Duckett to look over my list? Why would he have her look over my work?"

"Did you talk to him about it?"

"No not yet. I didn't want to overreact or jump to any conclusions. There's a chance that it's all a big coincidence and he's simply delegating some of the tasks."

"Yes, could be."

"But you and I probably know that it isn't a coincidence and that they're going to try to give me hell over this whole EEOC thing."`

"Probably are, I just want you to be careful. Things are more than likely exactly how they seem, but until you are sure you have to play it straight. Stay focused on the job you have to do. Don't get too caught up and do too much. Let's not assume the worst. By the way, what did Grassley say about the complaint?"

"They are almost finished writing it up. There is a 30 day default judgment in it."

"What does that mean?"

"It means that the school system would have 30 days to respond. If they don't, we win."

"Wouldn't it be nice if they didn't respond?"

"I suppose. The complaint should be ready tomorrow afternoon."

"You want me to take it and file it for you?"

"Are you sure that wouldn't be doing too much?" I knew that my sarcasm wasn't justified, but every once in a while my passion got the best of me. The stress of working every day in a place where I felt no support, made it so depressing I yearned for an outpouring of support when I got home. I recognized it as being unfair to Alexander, but still I found myself acting out at times.

"Relia, you know that I didn't mean it like that."

"Really, how did you mean it then?"

"Look, I've been on board this whole time. I've tried to support you and give you nothing but my honest opinion. I know it hurts. I know that you feel rejected by the people whom you've given your all to, but you have to realize that I'm on your side. I say what I say because I don't want you to get too overwhelmed or to cheat yourself out of anything. Now, I can take the complaint downtown and file it for you if you want me to. That I'll do. What I won't do is allow you to take your frustration out on me. I love you, but I'm not having it."

I picked at my food, like a scolded child. Alexander was right, and just that quickly he'd set me straight. "I'll call you when the complaint is ready. It would be nice if you took it downtown for me." Alexander smiled at me and went back to his meal. I smiled and quietly finished mine. I knew the remainder of the day would be peaceful. This wasn't always the case. This ordeal had managed to turn me into an emotional wreck. I kept my composure at work, but once I got home my frustration would overflow and spill over into my otherwise happy marriage.

I was bubbling with nervous excitement when I got the phone call that my complaint was ready. My trembling hands made it hard to turn the crisp pages. It became more and more real as I read the words on each page. The minute that this complaint crossed the clerk's counter, there would be no turning back. If the EEOC claim caused this much concern and perceived retaliation, what would filing the actual litigation initiation do? Still, I read through it with confidence and decided to forge ahead.

"Okay, you do realize that this step will be life changing, right?"

"Alexander, you know that I know that. I thought we decided that months ago."

"Sure we talked about it, but doing it is a whole different thing."

"Yeah, believe me. I'm scared to death. But Alexander, I have to do this. It's not really about me. It's more about breaking the mold and stepping outside of status quo."

"You always have wanted to be a trailblazer."

"I don't know about all that. I'm just trying to step out and dare to do the right thing."

"Okay. Let's do it baby."

"I guess." I handed the bound complaint to Alexander. Our hands touched as we paused each with one hand on the document. I said a quick prayer and used the other couple of seconds to wonder how I happened onto such a supportive man. I watched him in absolute awe as he left en route to the court house.

Though it was tough, I managed to refocus on work once Alexander left to file the complaint. I made major headway on developing my program to meet the needs of my students, and met with several of the parents of students whom I felt would possibly have academic or behavior problems. I began to feel like the little old lady who lived in the shoe. She had so many children (in my case with problems) that she did not know what to do. I made the decision to tap into my Mentor Program. I wanted each child who carried the label of being extremely at risk to have a person who would show that he or she cared about his or her future. As I looked at my list, I saw several students who fell into this category. Where would I possibly find this many people to be positive role models and take time out of their busy schedule to become involved with such a program? I had Alexander and Addison, my oldest son, and almost their entire office already with their hands full with assigned mentees. They had both agreed and several of the people at their office also had agreed to become involved. My target had been African American males, since they experienced the most difficulty, had the overwhelming dropout rates, displayed a lack of attendance, and experienced a shortage of positive role models in their homes and neighborhoods. After contacting other people I knew and getting other personnel at our school to participate, I had matched the number of mentors, finally, with the number of children in need.

I held an orientation meeting where I explained the program to the mentors. Each mentor received a folder with a child's name and grade. The folder also contained a list of words they could use to praise their child and suggestions regarding other activities they could use to help bring about success. My only request was that they meet with their mentees once every six weeks after the students had received their report cards, praising them for the good work and encouraging improvement for the not so good. I had already decorated a room at our school for the mentors and their mentees to have their six-week meetings. After the brief orientation to the program, I opened it up for questions, concerns and suggestions. This was followed by each mentor meeting with his or her mentee. We took individual pictures of each mentor and student and posted them in the Mentoring Room. Alexander provided pizza and soda for everyone.

This program was very successful, and a reporter thought it was newsworthy enough to visit our school and talk with the mentors about it. One mentor told how his student didn't have a phone. So he purchased envelopes, paper, and stamps so that he and his student would have a means of communication. Another mentor sent a beautiful bouquet of flowers to our school for her student's birthday. And another mentor bought an artist kit for his student. My mentors included business owners, bankers, judges, secretaries, real estate agents, engineers, attorneys, doctors, accountants, air line pilots and college students.

One particular name stood out in my paperwork. I was used to seeing the names of certain students over and over again. The absence of parental involvement tended to result in behavior issues that were almost always linked to academic progress. For this reason, I found that the same names that were identified as "at risk" were often on the "behavior issues" list as well as on the "academically challenged" list.

As I worked on my paperwork, I came across one of the names that seemed to fit this pattern. Sabrina Angela Johnson was often called "a holy terror". Even in elementary school, she had the manners of a caveman, the tongue of a sailor, and the potential to bring fear to the heart of any teacher. Yet I remember the very first time I laid eyes on her. She was a pretty girl, with deep eyes and amazingly deep dimples. Her hygiene was far from immaculate, and the minute she opened her mouth or began to act out, the beauty in her face would dissipate, overshadowed by the ugliness that she radiated. Seeing her name over and over on the "lists of serious behavior problems" caused my heart to go out to this young girl.

I pulled her cumulative record and began to look it over. I was unsure of what I was looking for or what piece of information I could find that would give me insight into her life, but the longer I looked, the clearer things became. The parental contact information we held on file for Sabrina Angela Johnson was for her mother. No father was listed. The lack of emergency contact information told the story. The daytime contact on file was a work number; the evening contact on file was also another work number. Ms. Johnson was a single mother who spent so much time working that she had very little time left to be a parent to Sabrina and her three siblings.

Because many of the crucial years of her early childhood development had passed, I wondered if there was any way that I could make a difference in Sabrina's life. Still, I felt that she deserved a chance to have a productive life. I made a mental note and moved on to the next thing on my to-do list.

"Knock, knock!" Mrs. Boatman, one of our high efficacy veteran teachers, had a habit of verbally knocking.

"Mrs. Boatman. Come on in. It's good to see you again. I didn't really see you during in-service."

"I was there; I just was doing a lot of running around. You know how unorganized administration can be at the beginning of the year."

"Do I! I've been dealing with that for years now."

"And of course when they are unorganized, it leaks right into our world as teachers. But I'm not complaining; I love what I do. Sometimes you just have to take the good with the bad."

"Well, you look good; it's good to see you."

"You too. I just thought I'd come by and see how you were doing. My class is in the library. Lord knows I needed that little break. So how was your summer?"

"It was fine. It just flew by." Though I considered Mrs. Boatman a close personal associate, almost a friend, I just wasn't ready to risk talking about how I spent my summer. There was too much at stake for me to gamble on anything. So I simplified my discussion of my summer activities, "I was actually ready to get back here though. What about you? Weren't you ready to come back to these new happy faces?"

"Oh, I must be honest. I wasn't. I could have used another couple of weeks. I really enjoyed spending that time with my girls. We had a really good summer."

"I bet. You always have had a really good relationship with your daughters. I just wish all of my students had that kind of relationship with someone at home." As I spoke, I talked myself into what I thought could be a step in the right direction for Sabrina. "You know, Mrs. Boatman, you should become a mentor."

"I don't know about that. I can barely manage my life the way it is. I'm not sure if I can handle any more responsibility."

"I know you're busy. We all are. I just think that you have a special gift when it comes to connecting with young girls. Take your students, for example. They always leave your classroom better students than they were when they entered. You have a way with them. I think you could make a big difference. Please, just one student."

"Ohhh," Mrs. Boatman was very hesitant. "Okay, but just one. We can do a trial run."

"Wonderful, it's Sabrina Angela Johnson. However, we can't do a trial run. You have to commit to it. If you don't see it through, it can do more harm than good."

"I know. I'm just not sure if I will be any help, especially to Sabrina. I've had a run-in or two with her and she is a bit of a handful. She called me an ugly white bitch just last week".

"Are you white? I never noticed." Mrs. Boatman and I both laughed. "No really! You have a way with the students that transcends the difference in race. I really believe you will have a positive effect on Sabrina. In fact, I know you can. We have to get her back on track before it's too late."

"Okay, what am I supposed to do?"

"Do what you do best. Just show that you care. Develop a relationship with her. We just want to expose her to a more productive way of life."

"Okay I'll think of something." Mrs. Boatman stood up with a deep sigh. She nodded in acknowledgement. "Something told me to go back to my classroom. I should have listened."

"Thank you Mrs. Boatman. I'll let Sabrina's mother and teacher know that you'll be mentoring her. You won't regret this. I promise. You're the best."

"Yeah, yeah. I'll keep you up to date." I wore a broad smile as I watched Mrs. Boatman leave and had a great feeling about her ability to work with Sabrina. If we were lucky, today could be the beginning of a brand new life for her.

Chapter 6   Retaliation

She spent days hiding out in the refuge of her home. She knew that returning to work would only put her back in the company of her offenders. Through many sleepless nights, she wondered what she could have done to draw such malice from her peers. Day after day, the wounds, buried beneath layers of out of season clothing, were hidden from her family. After being the family's example of strength for years, her own power and fortitude escaped her. The sun would rise and set, the world would continue to turn, yet her life stood at a standstill. Her rhythm was disrupted, her melody stolen.

The police knew the names of her attackers creating an expectation of a quick and somewhat painless turnaround. She awaited that call when the voice on the phone would say that she was safe and that every intruder was in custody. She planned to smile, nod, and just allow her life to get back to normal. Days turned to weeks and weeks turned to months, and still no call. There was never an update from the authorities. No one called and said, "We just wanted to let you know that we are still working your case and are dedicated to finding the people who did that to you."

The whole thing was quickly becoming exhausting and overwhelming. She finally made the decision to return to work. At work, it became very difficult to concentrate on the present as her thoughts were consumed with watching her back. Hair stood on the back of her neck each time one of the attackers walked by her and greeted her with a sarcastic "good morning". Even more unnerving were the staff meetings, where everyone involved——the victim, the attackers and their accomplices——shared a single space. The intruders sat and stared her down, waiting on her to break and run out of fear. Yet, she stood strong and walked every day in the face of her enemies.

Before long, the wait became too much, and she decided to call the detective who was scheduled to work her case. She was careful with her wording, trying desperately not to upset him. In her mind, he was her only ally. "Well, ma'am. We've been working the case and pursuing all of the leads that you provided. And we've run into a few dead ends. All of the people that you named in your report have alibis."

"That's not possible. I'm certain of who was there."

"Are you sure? Because they all had alibis."

"Of course they would. How easy is that? 'Let's just say that we were all together and be each others' alibis.' I know they were all together because they all took part in raping me."

"Maybe so, but we just haven't been able to find any proof of their guilt."

"What about the exam? I know the exam turned some things up."

"Yeah, there were some things that were suspicious, but so what?"

"So, what? What do you mean so what?"

"It doesn't prove that THEY did anything wrong. It shows a high likelihood that something happened to you that day, but the exam gave no indication that you were raped by those people."

"I'm stunned." She tried to even her shaky voice out and remain brave. "So what's next?"

"Well, we will keep working this case, and hopefully something will come up. In the meantime, feel free to do whatever you need to do to come to grips with this whole thing and hopefully get some healing."

At the end of her conversation with the detective, the tears flowed without restraint. She mourned the free spirit within her that died when she was raped. After a few days of living in sadness, she turned to her strength in God, opening up her Bible to read a few pages out loud. A new spirit materialized. She vowed to keep her hand connected to God's hand and continue her crusade with a driven mission.

CHAPTER 6

After filing my complaint with the courts, I assumed naturally that the 30 days would fly by. Just as the mortgage due date seemed to show up every month more quickly than expected, I assumed that the deadline for response would arrive before I knew it. Of course, things hadn't worked out that way, and the days of waiting became harder and harder to bear. With each day of mounting tension, I found myself more and more focused on justice, unmoved by the acts of retaliation that continued to brew in the workplace; meanwhile, my peace surfaced daily while working out at the fitness center.

"Okay ladies, one more set," echoed the words off the wall of mirrors, where we watched sweat roll down our cheeks and chests. "Think about the summer. Think about that swimsuit that you've wanted to get into or that pair of jeans that you can't button."

For me, fitness came as naturally as breathing. Not only was it a pasttime, it was a passion. Just as I strived every day to enhance the lives of my students, I got joy from seeing women transformed through fitness. Lately, however, fitness had been rescuing me from the tension of the case. I couldn't count the number of miles I ran in the 30 days that led up to the response deadline. This day was no different as I pushed the troubles out of my mind and concentrated even harder on the workout before settling into the long drive home and thinking about the case.

"Attorney Grassley, please," I said in a whisper. Tapping the wheel anxiously while waiting on him to come to the phone, I was excited about the possible outcome, yet nervous about this new milestone.

"Hello Attorney Grassley. This is Dr. Union. I was wondering if you'd heard anything yet. I wasn't sure if anyone had contacted you."

"No, I haven't heard anything. I'm surprised that I haven't heard back by now."

"So what happens if they don't respond? I know we have the default judgment, but how does that work? I know it isn't as simple as it sounds."

"No, you're right. It's not that simple. I'm not saying that on the 30th day if you haven't heard back, you can expect a check for a million dollars on day thirty one. The default judgment just gives you leverage and is an acknowledgement of the fact that you have diligently given them a chance to state their case. In the instance of our complaint, their silence is equivalent to guilt."

"But . . ." something told me that he was about to give me the fine print. "I know there's a but."

"But...it is up to the judge to enforce the default judgment clause."

"So you're saying that even if they do default, a judge would have to make them pay the money."

"Yes. But let's not even worry about that right now. Let's just wait and see if they respond."

"I guess you're right. I'll just wait and see what happens. I'll give you a call tomorrow." I hung up the phone; thinking about the "what ifs" involved in my case, just knowing there was a chance the school system could default with no consequence, made my head hurt.

That throbbing, needling headache kept me awake tossing and turning all night. With the impending deadline controlling my thoughts, sleep was out of the equation. A cup of warm cocoa sounded relaxing, so I moved from the bed to the kitchen quietly, cognizant of Alexander's need to rest.

"Can you make me one too?" asked Alexander, whose voice caught me by surprise.

"I'm so sorry. Did I wake you up?"

"Well, I wasn't really sleeping all that well. You just gave me even more reason to get up." I smiled at him lovingly. I was sure that he had no idea just how moved I was by this act of caring.

Cocoa mugs in hand, we snuggled on the sofa and quietly enjoyed each other's company. "I remember how nervous I was when I went away for school. I still don't think I could have done it without you." I began to try to let Alexander in on why this case was so important to me. I'd given up so much of me to prepare for a future in administration. I'd risked my family and my job to grow in the way that I thought was necessary for the future. Pursuing my doctorate and making a great effort to solve the problems that are prohibiting our children's positive future endeavors were major goals for me. So with Alexander's blessing, I proceeded with full steam ahead. I left my home and moved hours away on a fellowship. The days missing my husband seemed unbearable at times. No one could imagine the guilt that I felt every time I talked with my youngest son or helped with homework through a fax machine. I should have been there beside him, coaching him through his studies. A daily question haunted me -- was my pursuit selfish? Still, Addison, my oldest son, encouraged me to continue; so I endured. He would always share some of his Bible verses of encouragement. One of my favorite was from II Corinthians 12:9; when God said, "My grace is sufficient," and another came from I Corinthians 1:30; God said "I give you wisdom."

The loneliness of being so far from home with very few people whom I could relate to, distracted me from my purpose, yet I persevered. Making my family proud was the source of my fortitude and it gave the entire experience value. When I was finally done with the program, I marveled in an unbelievable feeling of pride. My marriage and family were still intact, and I had reached a major life and career milestone. The day that I heard "Dr. Relia F.Union" for the first time was the beginning of the next chapter in my life, or so I had thought.

"If I'm going to be held back because of my race, then the sacrifice was for nothing. The time away from you, the days of eating fast food, and the countless nights spent in the library were for nothing."

"Not exactly, Relia. I think that you accomplished the goal you set out to accomplish. You have your degree, the knowledge needed to help your students, and the respect and love of your family. Alexander had said it all and in one swoop had eased my mind. Now, I could capture the sleep that once evaded me.

The next morning, I felt a nervous feeling in my stomach because the deadline for the system to respond to my complaint had officially passed. To my knowledge, no response had been submitted. Just for confirmation, I decided to get Attorney Grassley on the phone. "Well, Dr. Union," he sounded as excited as I did. "The board has officially defaulted."

"Really?" I was still somewhat puzzled. "So you're telling me that they completely ignored the complaint. I don't remember there being a million dollar surplus in the budget. So they must know something that we don't know."

"Yes. Either that or they were caught off guard and unable to get things together in enough time to address it."

"Okay, so what's next?"

"Now we have to file the motion, demanding them to pay the default judgment amount. That usually moves pretty quickly. So it won't be long before we'll hear something. My paralegal is actually typing the motion up as we speak. I'll give you a call and let you know how things turn out."

"Great. Thanks for everything."

Though work was quickly turning into a hostile environment for me, my students were actually getting the benefit of it. Because the lines of communication between Mr. Williams and me had been almost severed, I found myself giving everything that I had to the students. Before, a certain level of bureaucracy required me to give almost half of my time to administrative tasks and paperwork. Now, as if to limit my power, Williams was slowly removing my responsibilities. In the past, Ms. Duckett and I had split up the social security paperwork. She handled the forms for her students, and I would handle the forms for mine. Suddenly, Ms. Duckett was placed in charge of the paperwork for all of the families, including mine. At first, it was tough watching the tasks that I was accustomed to doing be handed off. But soon, I took it upon myself to replace each task that was taken from me with my own personal projects: the students.

Sabrina Angela had been showing great progress under Mrs. Boatman's mentorship. In only a few weeks, her smile had become more frequent, and her teachers noted a significant improvement in her disposition. Tonya had made enough progress to be on the Second Honor Roll (all Bs and satisfactory conduct). Carl was adjusting well to his new home life and seemed to balance school and his home environment well. And John was receiving weekly school visits and gifts from his mentor. Just when I felt that I had a handle on my students, a new and more compelling encounter occurred. We were nearing the end of the semester when Charlotte Hope walked into my office, surly and shy. She had just revealed to her teacher that she was being molested by her stepfather.

"I told my mother," she spoke in a matter of fact tone, void of emotion. "She didn't do nothing about it. She got upset and told me I was lying." My heart went out to her as I searched for the words to comfort her. "I just can't take it no more. I know my family is gonna be mad, but I just can't take it no more."

"Charlotte, being a mother is a tough job. I'm sure that your mother loves you. She just made a mistake. But you did the right thing in telling us. Now, we're going to get you some help."

When social services came to talk with Charlotte, she freely shared the horrible events with the caseworker. No tears ran down her face, neither did she flinch nor stutter as she gave the report that would be used to investigate her claims. She sat strong, unfazed, and somewhat mature for her age. The caseworker took the time to explain to Charlotte that she would be temporarily removed from her home, until the investigation was completed. In many of the cases that I'd experienced, the child showed an unwillingness to be removed from the home in which they were being abused. Not Charlotte; she nodded in acknowledgement and asked only two questions. "Will I be able to stay at my school? How will I get to school?"

"Charlotte," I looked her in the eyes and assured her, "We will work something out. I will make sure you remain at your school and get to school every day." I will never forget that look of peace that she had on her face as she left my office that day. It mirrored the look that she wore on the day that social services came to the school to take her to her new foster home. Finally Charlotte, after years of living a nightmare, was rescued.

Just as Attorney Grassley had promised, our motion to declare the system in default moved quickly. However, the outcome was not what I expected. "Dr. Union, I'm afraid I have some bad news for you. The judge that has been assigned to your case refused to make the system pay the million dollars for defaulting."

"How can he do that? Doesn't that kind of defeat the purpose of having a default clause?"

"Well yes, but the judge has the right to uphold it. In this case, the judge refused to do so."

"Okay," my thoughts raced in anger. "So what's next?"

"Your next step should be to file a lawsuit."

"Okay. Let's do it."

"Well that's the thing. I don't think I'm a good fit for this case. For one, my firm doesn't have the greatest rapport with the judge assigned to your case. I think that my handling your case would further damage any chance that you have at getting fair treatment. I'm sorry. I think you have an opportunity at something great here, but it's going to be a long road. That's why I couldn't accept the case at the beginning. I needed to get a feel for what this case needed and what judge would be handling it. It looks like this is going to be a tough fight. You're going to need the best representation that you can get, and I can't say with confidence that my firm would fit your needs."

"I'm sorry to hear that. Can you recommend anyone? Do you have any colleagues who would be willing to handle it? I have already talked to dozens of attorneys, and no one has been willing to take on the system."

"Yes. I sort of expected that. I can give you a few more names, but…"

"I know, I know. You can't make any promises."

By the time my conversation with Attorney Grassley was over, all of the wind had been knocked out of me. My case was at a standstill, and I had no one willing to champion my cause.

Weeks and weeks of searching went by and still no attorney had accepted my case. Many called it a milestone case, others called it impossible, and some actually claimed not to see it as racial discrimination. I began to prepare to represent myself, pooling every resource I could to become fluent on historic precedents and legal jargon. I spoke to an associate of mine who was an attorney while we worked out. I checked out law books and spent hours and hours each night reading them line by line. As the deadline for filing the lawsuit loomed, I felt that I was as ready as I could be, but not nearly ready enough. Again, Alexander insisted that taking on federal court would be a bit more than I could chew on. Feeling as if it were my only option, I continued to try to prepare.

Then the day before the deadline, my miracle occurred. After all his persistence, Alexander found me the perfect attorney. Mary Edelman was an African American lawyer who was excellent in federal law and heaven-sent. When Alexander called me about her, I dropped everything and went to meet with her. I nervously shared my case and documentation with her. I spoke quickly as if the deadline was minutes rather than hours away. An hour after meeting her and sharing my documentation with her, Mary eagerly agreed to jump on the case, immediately got to work, and we filed the lawsuit on the day of the deadline.

"Okay, Dr. Union. We filed the suit, but there is still a ton of work to do and a long bumpy road ahead of us. We are missing a lot of documentation. I've looked over the information that was submitted to the EEOC, and without a doubt, they did not do a thorough investigation. We have to get the pertinent information essential to proving your case. In this information, we really don't have a clear case of racial discrimination."

"What do you mean?"

"Well, in looking at the typed scores that were originally submitted, you and Amy performed almost equally in the interviews. As a matter of fact, according to this, a couple of other candidates scored well, also. So we can't base our case off this alone."

"I understand."

"Because these are not the raw scores, we have to find other pieces of evidence to support our claim. I know it's hard, but I want you to go home and relax. I will take care of everything, and I will call you if I need anything." I walked away from my meeting with Mary feeling revived.

My lawsuit had been filed and I had my heroine. I was able to try to settle back into a normal routine as a counselor. Carl's story began to spread, and he soon became an inspiration to others. His living conditions were found to be deplorable, yet he remained committed to his education. He had the responsibilities of an adult and carried them with a positive outlook. As a result, I nominated him for the "The Young Heroes Award". The entire school was in a frenzy of support behind Carl. As the date of the awards ceremony approached, I called him to my office to make sure that he was prepared.

"So Carl, are you excited about the ceremony?"

"Yes Ma'am."

"Do you need anything to prepare for it?"

"Well, yes Ma'am. Maybe a suit."

"I'm sure we can handle that. We are all so proud of you. I just want to let you know that we are all behind you. It doesn't matter who wins. Just the fact that so many people think of you as a role model is a huge deal. I'm just proud to have you as one of my students. You will grow up to be a great man!" Carl blushed deeply as I complimented him. He seemed unfamiliar with compliments and was unsure of how to respond. "Thank you." He was always short and to the point, and today was no different.

When the day of the reception arrived, Carl looked like a handsome prince. His suit fit him perfectly, and he beamed with pride in it. He had a fresh haircut, compliments of one of his former teachers. Hearing Carl's name announced as the winner and watching him be awarded $5,000.00 will always be one of the proudest moments of my career. He gave the most intelligent and heart warming presentation I have heard by such a young person. As I looked around the room, I saw tears rolling down the faces of many of the people. People of all races came forward to offer Carl any type of help to assist him on his road to success. One lady offered to purchase any school supplies that he might need. A couple of young men offered him an all-expenses paid adventure camping trip. The offers continued to pour in during and after the ceremony. I am certain that Carl's life changed that day. He realized that there was value and honor in doing the right thing.

It also launched a new initiative in my mind, the need to spotlight those students who did what they were supposed to do. These were the average students who didn't make the Honor Rolls, but were a joy for every teacher to work with. They often fell between the cracks if their behavior didn't garner them negative attention. If Carl's home life had not been brought to light, he would have been one of those students. He was an average student with good behavior and a commendable attitude. I made it my mission to show other students just like him that they too were appreciated and that their efforts did not go unnoticed.

As the end of the year approached, news of my lawsuit began to leak out, and the alienation became more apparent. I handled it well for the most part and managed to keep my overall focus on doing the job that I was paid to do. However, things came to a head when a petty attempt at alienating me spilled over to my students. To increase knowledge about Fire Prevention, Ms. Duckett arranged a large field trip to the Fire Museum. As the word spread about this trip, my students' excitement began to grow; they assumed that they would be allowed to attend the museum as well.

I was told however, that my students would not be able to go. No justification was offered to support this decision. It was not due to a shortage of funds or any budgeting issues; I was just told that they could not go. It hurt me to have to tell my kindergarten through second grade students that they couldn't participate. I even felt a little guilty because clearly they were being affected by the resentment the administration felt towards me.

Mr. Williams also reduced my involvement in the most important activity of the school year, standardized testing. This was a major undertaking that required diligent management and precise planning. Just when the time came for the committee to begin working on the tests, I was informed that Ms. Duckett would be taking care of it on her own. It was extremely important and far too technical for one person alone to handle, but again, it was just another step towards alienating me and minimizing my ability to provide value.

Next, my spelling bee responsibility was also handed over to Ms. Duckett. I was no longer allowed to sponsor or support my students or drive them to the different schools where the spelling bees took place. Those steps, however, were small in comparison to the next blow.

It was May and again, we were preparing to close out another school year. I'd resorted to spending the majority of my day in my office making sure that every detail in my reports was accurate and in line. Because I was under constant scrutiny, I felt increased pressure to ensure that I produced excellent work. "Dr. Union," I received a call from the office. "Mr. Williams would like to see you in his office."

"I'll be right there." I gathered my pen and yellow legal pad quickly and headed to his office, anxious to know what he could possibly want to meet with me about. When I entered, he was sitting at his desk, with his back straight and a very serious look on his face. His body language contradicted his expression, however. His hands were nervously tapping the desk, and his eyes never made contact with mine. I decided to mirror him and put on my best poker face. I sat in a chair directly in front of him with my back straight and my face as professionally stern as I could muster.

"Dr. Union, it has been a joy working with you these years. As you know, we were able to save your position last year. Well, I really hate to tell you this, but you have been declared surplus."

"Excuse me? What do you mean declared surplus?"

"In our last meeting, we talked about the budgeting issues that we were having."

"Yes, but we also were supposed to have a follow-up meeting to discuss budgeting and our options. If I'm not mistaken, that meeting never happened."

"Dr. Union, please don't make this any harder than it has to be. I respect you. You are a great counselor, and I think it will be a shame to lose you. But right now, the budget is tight, and we were forced to make some tough decisions. You should have no problem transitioning to another school. Of course, I plan to write a letter of recommendation on your behalf, expressing how invaluable you have been to this school."

Completely stunned, I exited Mr. Williams's office knowing that he had just fed me a line of crap. I was being moved because of the stand that I was taking against the system. It didn't matter how invaluable I was; I had officially been blacklisted, I gave Mary a call. "Mary, I know that all of these things are no coincidences.

"Oh, I'm sure they're not. But I can't lump those in with the suit that we've already filed. That is another case in itself."

"So what do I do about it?"

"You need to file this with EEOC. We still have to finish developing your original case; we are almost there. In the meantime, keep very detailed and accurate records of everything that you're experiencing. Continue with your career as if none of this is happening. Once we get to the point where we can be certain that this is in fact retaliation, you'll have to start the process over."

"You mean…"

"Yes, the EEOC. They would first have to investigate it, and then we would go from there."

"But we know that the EEOC isn't going to give it a second look. You see how they handled my first claim."

"I know, but they are the first point of contact. Just trust me. You're doing a great job. Hang in there. I told you this road would be long and bumpy. This is just one of the bumps. First work on finding another school and then take this summer and regroup. Continue down your career path as if none of this were going on."

Mary's advice made sense, and I was determined to follow it. They would not be given my permission to wear me down. The school system was in this thing for the long haul, but so was I.

Chapter 7   The Conspiracy

The conspiracy slowly began to make sense. Not only were the authorities not trying to find out the truth in her case, but they seemed to be trying to conceal it. However, she wouldn't be ignored. She pushed and pushed, holding the authorities accountable for each and every aspect of her case. As she faced her accusers daily at work, she started holding her head up and looking them squarely in the eyes. Hiding and ducking had become tiresome, and she made her mind up that she was not to be intimidated any longer.

Finally, after over four years of pretending to investigate her attack, the police indicted some of her attackers. The prosecution was hasty, and after waiting what seemed like forever for results, she was rushed onto a stand to testify about what happened that day. The prosecutor was strategically gentle and asked all of the questions that were needed to give the jury a descriptive picture of the rape. She spoke of her pain and the anxiety that she experienced in facing her accusers every single day at work. She talked about the whispers among her attackers. The tension in the room mounted when the questions led to the attack.

"Did you scream? Did you say no?"

"Yes, I screamed. I screamed as loudly as I could, but nobody stopped. They just kept pushing and switching places. Two would hold me down while the next person had his or her way. I kept praying for someone to come to my rescue and to do something to stop this. I just didn't understand how so many people could stand for this repulsive crime to occur to another human being. -

"Are you sure about who attacked you?"

"Yes, I'm sure."

"Are they here?"

"Yes, some of them are."

"Can you point to them?" She leaned forward poised with quiet confidence and looked each attacker in the eye. She pointed sternly and strongly, calling them by their first and last names as she pointed. There was no doubt in her mind, and she wanted the jury to know that. The prosecutor wrapped up his examination and had a seat. Just when the anxiety of testifying began to settle, the defense attorney stood and began his attack.

"So you actually expect these intelligent men and women of the jury to believe that you were raped in a classroom full of people with whom you'd spent over 20 years working?"

"Yes, because it's true."

"Furthermore, is it your testimony that you screamed, and no one else in the entire building heard you?"

"Well, I can't say if anyone heard me or not. I just know that I screamed, and nobody came to help."

"Why you?"

"Excuse me?"

"Why would they want you of all people? You'd spent years working along side of them. Anyone in their situation would know that you would have no problem identifying them. So why would so many hard-working educators put their lives on the line for a quick round with you?"

"I don't know. They'll have their turn up here soon. You should ask them?"

"I'm asking you." The prosecutor stood.

"Your honor, I object. That question calls for speculation on her part."

"Sustained, sustained." The judge repeated drawing attention to her ominous presence. *"You may disregard the question."*

"Now, don't get me wrong. No-one here is saying that you weren't attacked. I am just unclear on how you are the only one who knows about this massive, group rape. Are you aware that there was absolutely no evidence that confirms that any of these people were guilty of attacking you? Even when you were seen by the doctor, there was no DNA linking any of these people to your attack."

"I know what happened, and I know who did it. I don't know why. I did not do anything to encourage their actions. I have done nothing but come to work every day and try to make sure that my students receive my best. I did not deserve to be draped across a desk and invaded by people whom I thought respected me. What I'm not so sure of is why everyone is working so hard to cover this injustice and make me look like the bad guy."

"Well, they do not have to work too hard to do that. The evidence speaks for itself."

"Your honor, I object. Counsel is merely badgering the witness. How is she supposed to testify when he isn't asking questions?" The judge took a deep breath as if frustrated by the defense attorney. "Objection sustained. Please get to the point, Counsel. You're pushing your luck."

"Your honor," the defense attorney said boldly sneering, as his eyes drilled a disgusting nail into her. "I have no further questions." She sat still on the witness stand. Her head was spinning, and her ears burned with embarrassment. Though she tried to maintain her composure, the expressions of the jury gave no hints as to whether she had accomplished that. "Thank you. You are excused and may leave the stand."

The walk back to her seat seemed miles long. Just as she was about to sit down, her stomach changed the plan, and a wave of nausea came over her. She rushed out of the room with her hand over her mouth and away from all the intimidating faces.

CHAPTER 7

"So how are you getting settled in at the new school?"

"You know me; I always make my students a priority, but I just can't keep doing the same thing. It's getting to be too much for me. My children's stories are getting sadder and sadder. Their needs are getting greater and greater, while my belief of adding value on a larger scale is diminishing."

"Now, how could you say that? You are one of the more valuable assets in that whole school system. And I'm not just saying that as your paid attorney. I really believe that. I listen to your ideas for these children and the pride that you have when you talk about them. How can you say your belief of adding value is diminishing?"

"Mary, it's kind of like this. You practice law every day right?"

"Right."

"And what is your long term career goal?

"Well, any lawyer worth his or her salt wants to become a partner in his or her firm. So I guess that would be my goal-- becoming a partner and then a judge."

"And have you set a time limit for when you'd like to accomplish that?"

"Most definitely."

"Okay, so let's say that the time limit you set was to come and go and you still hadn't made partner. Yet, all around you, your peers, colleagues, associates, and even those who are less qualified than you were passing you by and reaching levels and heights that you had yet to attain. Wouldn't you at some point start to question the value that you were bringing to the firm?"

"I most certainly would. Especially with what you have encountered, I would be highly upset. I guess that's why I was so anxious to take your case. I can truly understand your pain. I just hate that you doubt the value that you are adding. What about the kids? You know you're a blessing to them."

"Yeah, but I wanted to be a blessing to them in more than just one capacity."

"So what is the latest occurrence?"

"Well, I took your advice and applied for every administrative position in the system where I met the requirements that are listed. I have received notices that they have my résumé. However, they have not scheduled me for any interviews. They have just been ignoring me ever since they transferred me."

"And? What did they say?"

"I told you: nothing. Now I know competition is tight but it's not that tight. I applied for a P.E. curriculum administrative position, and I didn't even get an interview for that. I mean, come on. Physical Fitness is central to my life. Now, how did I not get an interview for that position? Just a minute Mary," I said as I pulled a letter from my folder. "Please read this letter out loud that I recently received from Human Resources."

Mary read the letter aloud, "Dear Relia Union, We find that you have met the Highly Qualified requirements in the areas of Elementary K-6. Our records indicate your scores on the Praxis specialty tests meet the standards of Federal No Child Left Behind requirements."

"Well, did you remember what we talked about? Make sure that you go through the whole process."

"Yeah. I actually ran into one of the many highly paid assistant superintendents at an open house the other day. I cornered him, and you should have seen how nervous he looked. He has ignored all of my calls and e-mails. He would have said anything to get rid of me."

"And what did he say?"

"He told me that I needed to speak with Deputy Superintendent Smith. He rushed me over to her as fast as he could. We had an appointment to meet last week. Can you believe this? She allowed me to make the trip to the administrative building, wait 25 minutes in her secretary's office, sit down in a chair in her office, and then she told me that she couldn't meet and needed to reschedule."

"No she didn't! That is so unprofessional and just-"

"Tacky?"

"Well, I was going to try to hold my tongue, but since you said it, yeah it's real tacky. It's a waste of your time.

"What's worse, she has scheduled and rescheduled me four other times. Oh by the way, I was just told that Mr. Williams got his dream school, the one he has been trying to get for years. What a pleasant coincidence. Furthermore, Amy got a principal position, and the system is not going to post her director position. Now you understand why I am tired and have had enough".

"So you know what's next, right?"

"Yeah, yeah. I know what's next."

Even though I knew what I needed to do long before I talked to Attorney Edelman, I still couldn't help but sigh in absolute dread of the next step. As much as I hated it, I had to bring attention to the retaliation that I was facing because of my lawsuit- even while we were waiting to hear word on my pending lawsuit. The thought of stirring up some more confusion made me uneasy. Therefore, I hoped that my meeting with Deputy Superintendent Smith went well. I needed to leave her office feeling that I had a chance of being treated fairly within the system and that I wasn't being targeted for exercising my constitutional rights. Sure, it was a long shot, but nearly a month later, I showed up prepared to meet, hoping for a great outcome.

After I was led into Deputy Superintendent Smith's office, she and I took seats at a small table. Instead of my résumé or personnel file, she had a small steno book in her hand. Suddenly, that gnawing feeling that this meeting would be no different from the others surfaced. My hunch was confirmed when she sat back in her chair and began the meeting in a nonchalant tone.

"And how may I help you?"

"Well, I have applied for several positions for which I met the qualifications listed on the job postings. However, I have not been granted a single interview. Assistant Superintendent Bently told me that you were the person whom I needed to discuss it with."

Smith crossed her arms as if bored and replied, "And what exactly do you want to discuss?"

"I was hoping that you could inform me of anything that I may be doing that is hindering me from advancing."

"Maybe it's your interview skills that are keeping you from being selected."

"No, I think you may have misunderstood. I have not received the opportunity to interview. I apply, they send confirmation that they received my submission, and then nothing happens. I've applied for over 14 positions, and it's been the same thing. Would you like to see my résumé?"

"Sure." I handed her the résumé and watched as she gave it a quick but critical scan. "I see you have your doctorate in Curriculum, Instruction and Policy Study. That's what I plan to get mine in. Well for one, you don't have much time in the classroom."

"I have five years as an elementary teacher, and I did several years of substitute teaching while working on my degree in elementary education. And I have my certification in administration and supervision—-more than enough qualifications for the position. As a matter of fact, I can think of several people who have received a position as principal or assistant principal who have no teaching experience. I am specifically referring to individuals who received alternative licensures."

"I'm sure you can."

"I'm not trying to be presumptuous," I continued, ignoring her attempt at sarcasm. "And I realize that every case is different, but I just can't understand how the classroom time would be an issue."

"I'm not saying that it is the issue. I'm only making an observation based on your résumé. That, in addition to being imprecise about the dates of the schools you have served, could affect how your résumé is received." As she talked, my mind flashed to the incomplete and unprofessional résumé of Amy.

"During the times that I served these schools, I was serving four schools simultaneously. That is why the dates are all the same."

I watched her lips move but ignored most of what she was saying. I was so over her, and so as politely as I could, I cut in to say, "Thank you so much for your time."

"Oh believe me, it was no problem." She stood on cue, and I made a quick exit from her office. Steam smothered my neck under my collar the entire way home. I couldn't wait to tell Alexander how she had behaved. When I rushed through the door of my house, all of the men in my life were sitting in our family room. Addison, was the first to greet me. "Whoa Mom, where's the fire? I know what that look means. Mom's upset." said Addison.

"Hello to you all, too." I replied unable to hide my frustration. "How was your day? Mine wasn't all that great. Thanks for asking. I am just confused about how our own people are not concerned about our children's future. Everyone that I have spoken with about my situation has been an African American in high ranking position. They know the struggle of an African American's road to self-improvement. They know our students need people who are qualified. Heck, even George W realized that. Being "Highly Qualified" was one of the main requirements of his No Child Left Behind Act." Addison quoted one of his favorite scriptures to clarify my confused state of mind.

"Mom, remember that God says: 'I will direct your steps.' Proverbs 3:5-6."

"Well, honey." Alexander couldn't resist the chance to get in on the action. "We haven't asked yet."

"Well, you should. You should ask me how my day was."

"Okay mother." Roman spoke up quickly. "How was your day?"

"It was horrible. I'm ready to retire. I have tried to hang in there through this oppression, but I am tired of it, and I give up. It is not worth it." Addison once again stated one of his favorite Bible scriptures.

"Mom, you feel it is not worth it. God says: 'It will be worth it.' Romans 8:28."

"Okay baby. Slow down. Tell us what happened."

"I had the meeting with Deputy Superintendent Smith today. I don't know why I went in there expecting her to be any different from the rest of those idiots I met with. Do you know that she had the nerve to tell me that I haven't gotten any interviews because I don't have enough teaching experience."

"Isn't that the same Deputy Superintendent Smith who was given a job by her cousin who just happens to be Superintendent Smith?"

"I know! Amy Folder didn't have any teaching experience. I can't tell you how many principals and assistant principals there are in the school system who have fewer years than I do, especially those who have an alternative licensure.

"Alternative licensure?"

"A type of licensure involving those people who have degrees in other fields. They decide they want to become an educator, after which they are rushed through a program and end up with limited training. Their first year is a do-or-die situation. Many of them and their students usually end up failing.

Then when she saw that excuse wasn't going to fly, she just sat and picked over my résumé. She stated that my résumé would be better received if I was more specific about the dates of the schools I have served."

"The dates of the schools you have served?" Addison, began to mirror my frustration. "Everybody knows this is not about your résumé."

"I feel all alone in this fight. I am not asking for anything special. I have paid my dues."

"Mom, you say: 'I feel all alone.' God says: 'I will never leave you or forsake you.' Hebrews 13:5."

"Addison, you are so good with your scriptures, and each one of them is right on time."

"Did you talk to the attorney today, baby? What did she say about all of this?"

"Yes. I talked to her. She said that she's still waiting on the judgment. She said that I should go through the entire process of trying to get another position. If they continue to ignore my submissions then I can file the retaliation claim with the EEOC."

"Okay Mom, we hate to run, but Roman is riding with me today, and he has a study session. But I say you should file the claim and stay on those people. If you ask me, none of it makes any sense. And remember, Mom, you may feel like you can't do it. However, God says: 'You can do all things.' Philippians 4:13." stated Addison as they left.

"All right. It was good to see you guys. Study hard Roman." I kissed them both and walked them out to the car. Before he got in the car, Roman gave me a hug and whispered in my ear. "Just remember Mom, it's really not you; it's them with the problem. Don't let them change who you are." I smiled at Roman; he'd always been so compassionate. "Thanks honey. I'll remember it. Be careful." I couldn't help but feel a slight shift in my mood as I walked back in the house. Yes, I was still irritated about the situation but not nearly as angered now by the meeting with Deputy Superintendent Smith.

Though the feeling of burnout was only increasing with each passing day, staying engaged with my students kept me going. But even that became harder and harder with each promotion for which I was looked over, observing as the people around me began to advance in their careers and still I sat stagnant, hindered by the vengeance from the administration. The last straw came when I noticed another one of my students going through life-changing turmoil.

A certain pain hits your heart when you see the innocence of a child being snatched away right before your eyes. To try to bring attention to child molestation, I presented a program entitled "Why Are You Touching Me?" I wanted to educate my students on the difference between appropriate and inappropriate touching. I expected to reap results later rather than sooner, so imagine my surprise when nine-year-old Kaylee walked into my office ready to open up. She told me of how her stepfather had been touching her and her six-year old sister in every single way that we discussed in the program. She'd been uncomfortable with it for a while but just wasn't sure if it was in fact wrong, or what to do about it. The program gave her the courage to let me know what was going on. Listening to her broke my heart. After years of seeing children be abused and neglected by people who were charged with loving and caring for them, I began to feel the pressure.

It didn't take long for the investigation to prove that her mother's husband had indeed molested Kaylee and her younger sister. When social services spoke with Kaylee's mother and informed her that the investigation supported the claims, she seemed less than remorseful, almost indifferent about the claim. To keep Kaylee and her younger daughter in her care, the mother had to separate from the stepfather and attend parenting classes to learn how to protect her children. Much to my chagrin, she refused to fulfill either requirement and instead settled for losing custody of Kaylee and her sister.

While at first it seemed that Kaylee was handling the conflict and turmoil of her life well, it didn't take long for the pain to set in. Only months into arriving at my new school, I was dealing with a suicidal Kaylee. At such a young age, the pain of the world had diminished her desire to live. Just as I was trying to cope with my own situation, her teacher rushed into my office with a note from this sweet girl. It read, *"Everyone has a mama but me. This makes me sad. All I want is to be with my mama. I don't want to live."* Suddenly, I wanted to be that mom she needed, but I couldn't take that pain away. I launched into action and worked to save what was left of Kaylee's life, but for me as an elementary counselor, it was the hardest of times. Our school psychologist immediately met with Kaylee and her sister. They both received one-on-one counseling and were placed in a foster home.

Before long, I decided that it was time to file another claim and look for a change of scenery. Filing the claim was easier this time around. I already had the information from the first claim and only needed to add to it the details regarding the retaliation. Because I had become so familiar with the process, I'd been very careful along the way to hold on to any piece of evidence that pertained to my case. The caseworker currently assigned to my case was more helpful than the last and seemed dedicated to investigating it thoroughly. I was hoping that this one would come through for me. My first caseworker never attempted to contact any of the witnesses listed on my form. He just kept repeating that the board stated that they have not done anything wrong. In the meantime, I decided to explore my career options.

The first option that I explored was retirement. "Maybe," I told the retirement benefits administrator, "it's time for me to walk away from the school system." Her response was "Here lately we are losing a lot of our good teachers." I took the retirement packet home and decided to talk the whole thing over with Alexander.

"So, are you really ready to retire?" Alexander questioned, looking me straight in the eyes. "Or are you just frustrated with them and ready for something different?"

"Well, I know I can't keep going to work feeling like this. Something is going to have to give. I guess I'm just ready for something different to happen. But you and I both know it's not going to happen, so why should I wait on that?"

"I just don't want you to make a move out of impatience or frustration. What about your lawsuit? Don't you think you should at least wait to see how that turns out?"

"The system is prolonging this situation. We don't know how long it'll be before we hear something back on that."

"Yeah, but don't you think you owe it to yourself at least to wait until that is resolved."

"Alexander, I really need a change of scenery. They have me trapped in this one position. It's taking a toll on me."

"Well, maybe you should look for a change of scenery. Look baby, I don't have all the answers. You have to do what makes you happy. I just want to try to be that voice of reason that we all need sometime. After that, it's up to you. I mean look at you, you're brilliant. I am absolutely sure that you'll figure it out, and you'll do what's best for you and your students."

Meanwhile, the peace and relaxation that a brisk run usually brought crossed my mind. With each mile, I pondered my situation and the dread that I was beginning to feel concerning my career. As if they knew that my thoughts were elsewhere, my workout partners pushed hard that day and were more attentive to each other. This allowed me to sit back as a participant and not push as hard as I usually do in the instructor's role. This workout was for me.   Inhale Relia. Get out of my life stress! With every lap, my mind began to clear, and the fog started to lift.

Once my workout was over, I was close to a decision. I couldn't wait to share my excitement with Alexander and called him immediately after I got in the car. I told him that it all became clear: I wasn't ready to retire. I'd been absorbing a great amount of anxiety because of the lawsuit, and it was starting to make me feel neurotic; as if I had to get out of the situation; I was ready to run away. Fortunately, all those years of training and a few miles of intense "physical therapy" had made it all clear. I just needed a change of scenery, and I knew exactly how to get it. I decided that if I couldn't be promoted into administration at this time, I would transfer and change the age group of children whom I worked with. It would provide me with the renewal that was so desperately needed at this point. Alexander seemed impressed and on board with the plan, and I hung up from our call believing that I'd made the right choice.

It didn't take long to find the school that became the transfer of my choice. I interviewed with the principal, who appeared to be very impressed with my programs. The transfer went through quickly, and just when things were really getting to be unbearable, I had that change that I'd been searching for. Only a couple of days after beginning at my new urban school, I got the call from my attorney. "We received Summary Judgment." She sounded melancholy and a little disappointed. "Summary Judgment, what does that mean?"

"Well, it's a final decision by the judge that resolves the lawsuit in favor of the school system. It means that the school system motion marshals all the evidence in their favor, compares it to our evidence, and argues that a reasonable jury looking at the same evidence could only decide the case one way--in favor of the system. If the judge agrees, which he did, then a trial would be unnecessary, and the judge enters judgment for the moving party, which is the school system."

"I should have expected that. They have their hands on everything around here. So what's next?"

"Well, next we appeal."

"And how long does that take?"

"Well, it's tough to tell. Sometimes it moves quickly, other times it can take years."

"Years?"

"Relia, I thought you were mentally prepared for a battle. I told you that this wasn't going to be easy. We can quit now, or we can appeal and keep trying to push ahead. It's your fight, so it's up to you."

"No, don't get me wrong. I don't want to quit, I'm just ready to get this over with. I don't think it really hit that this could be drawn out so long. It's been more than five and a half years so far. I definitely want to keep going. It's justice that I'm after, and if we have to fight to get it, so be it."

"Okay, so let me get to work on the appeal. How is everything else?" I updated Mary on the retaliation claim that I filed with the EEOC, and how the transfer had proven to be just what I needed. In light of the behavior that I'd been subjected to since filing the suit, Mary thought that the events done in retaliation needed to be worked into the lawsuit. The injustice was not just in the original act of racial discrimination but also in the cruel acts that followed, bringing attention to the injustice. We were in full agreement and started working towards our goal.

Attorney Edelman and I decided to take our time and make sure that the appeal included everything that we needed to make a stronger case. At the same time, the EEOC seemed to be investigating my retaliation claim a little more efficiently than they did the last claim. The lines of communication were more open with Mr. Hardy, the caseworker who was handling the retaliation case. He called regularly with updates and was willing to answer my questions freely. Though he was unable to say so, he seemed to believe in my claim. He was tied, however, by his obligation to the EEOC and even to the school system as well.

"Mr. Hardy, this is Relia Union. I was just calling to see if you had a new update for me?"

"No Ma'am. We don't really have anything new right now. Things are kinda on hold right now. You know, out of respect for the whole situation."

"What situation?"

"I'm surprised that you didn't read about it in the papers. Gregory Wallace, one of your administrators, suffered a heart attack and died instantly in his office."

"Yes. I heard about that. I guess I just don't understand what that has to do with my case."

"Well, it doesn't directly affect your case. But they do have a kind of ironic connection."

"What's that?"

"We were out there right before he died. We were questioning him about your case. We rode him kind of hard. I could see him sweating, but I just stuck with the script. I mean, I wasn't torturing him or anything, but I didn't take it easy like I think he expected me to."

"That is strange."

"I know that I have a job to do and that there isn't anything that I could have done, but I can't help but feel bad about it all."

"I want to let you know how much I appreciate your being so open and communicative about all of this."

"Oh, I'm just doing my job."

"It really helps that you are actually working my claim and not merely sweeping it under the rug. That's been going on long enough. Now, I know a certain level of confidentiality has to be maintained, so I won't hold you too long or try pressuring you too much. I just want to know that you're going to do the right thing here, regardless of how tough things may get along the way."

"Yes Ma'am," Mr. Hardy still sounded a little disturbed by everything. "I'll call you if anything else comes up."

I was feeling sad about the situation but unmoved about how it all happened. My case was not the only case of mistreatment of personnel that Wallace was involved in. A retaliation lawsuit filed against him by another teacher had actually made the headlines. This particular teacher cooperated with an investigation that involved cheating and another teacher who had fathered a child with a student and tried to arrange an abortion for her. The teacher who filed the suit was not only aware of these scandals; she also had inside information pertaining to the many years that teachers had been taking college entrance exams for the athletes. Shortly after she gave this information, she was transferred from her school of eleven years to a school where she was unable to carry out her teaching objectives. Meanwhile, the teacher who fathered a child with a student was allowed to continue teaching and complete a successful career. The teacher suing was left with only the unfulfilled desire to return to her school where she had spent her entire career.

I soon found out Wallace's fate brought a whole new meaning to my case. For some, the injustice was so strong that the guilt weighed on them like a ton of rocks. Even for those who felt guilt and remorse, the school system's power held them within the tight confines of their status quo. As educators, the counselors, and teachers struggled to provide the students with sound learning environments and opportunities to thrive and become outstanding members of society. Somewhere along the line, politics took the front seat, and the needs and education of the students took the back seat. Conspiracy and bureaucracy began to reign such that those people who started with wide-eyed excitement had grown into major pieces of the puzzle. Even when the pressure was on to own up to the damage and make it right, some still rejected the truth, even if doing so cost them more than they ever expected to give.

Chapter 8   Black on Black Crime

After a short recess, the trial resumed. The prosecutor called the ringleader to the stand and began a very harsh cross-examination. "So how long have you been in the field of education?"

"Just under 25 years."

"And how would you say that your career is going?"

"Well. It's been fine until now. I wouldn't exactly call being accused of rape as the highlight."

"So for the most part you would say that you've been happy in your career."

"Yes."

"So why would you risk throwing it all away by raping a colleague?"

The defense attorney jumped to his feet and strongly objected. The judge sustained causing the witness to slip a sly smile at the prosecutor, who took a second to gather his thoughts before continuing. "Is it true that you were in the vicinity on the day of the attack?"

"Yes."

"We've established that there was no staff meeting going on that day. Why were you there instead of at your office?"

"I had a meeting with my director."

"Would that be the same director who is joining you as a defendant?"

"Yes."

"Is there anyone other than you and the other defendants who can validate this so-called meeting between you and your director?"

"No."

"How about the secretary? She testified that she usually maintains the calendar. Did she have any knowledge about this so-called meeting?"

"No. She didn't schedule this particular meeting."

"So," the prosecutor paused, moving back towards his seat. "We're supposed to take your word for it?"

"I suppose."

"The police photographed you two days after the attack, and you had what appeared to be defensive scratches. How did you say that you received them?"

"I didn't say. They didn't ask. But if you must know, I got them doing some yard work. I trimmed the hedges, pared my shade tree, and dragged the branches to the curb. I must have scratched myself on some of the branches. "

"Must have? Are you sure about that?"

"Yes. I'm sure."

"Of course you are. I have one more question. How would you describe your relationship with your accuser?"

"Strictly professional."

"Of course you would. I have no more questions your honor." The prosecutor walked confidently to his seat.

She looked on from the crowd, unsure of whether the prosecutor had anything to be proud of. He hadn't proven anything in his cross-examination. At most, he may have cast a suspicious shadow on the defendants. There she sat, reliving the details of the event with every witness and every question. She felt pangs of fear when the clothing she wore that day was shown as evidence. She remembered hearing every tear and rip in the suit on the day that it occurred. She closed her eyes and began to recall every painful second in her mind. Truly, her life would never be the same. She looked at the faces of the defendants, hoping to see some sign of remorse. There was none. Rather, they only dug in deeper and salted the wounds left from the attack.

Once in a while, she found herself having to excuse herself from the court room. Listening to the details would become overwhelming causing her to feel sick to her stomach. Yet she overcame and would return to sit *through more character assassination. It felt as if it wasn't her attackers on trial, but rather her character that was being prosecuted. All of this would have been fine if the outcome was certain. From the looks of things, however, the outcome was anything but certain.*

CHAPTER 8

"I don't think it's a money issue; we have enough money." I found myself discussing a very familiar topic with one of the teachers, many of whom felt the strain of working in this ill-managed system. They often came and vented to me about the stress that they faced everyday. "The problem is in how it's being managed."

"That, Dr. Union," Mrs. Collins paused from stirring her coffee to point at me. "That is the issue. They require the teachers to be qualified, excuse me highly qualified, but the administration and the board members are not held to any level of accountability. They can mismanage funds and make decisions that negatively affect the education of our students."

Mrs. Collins' statements struck home with me, which was the main reason the lawsuit had to be filed. Still, no matter how comfortable I seemed to be with my peers and co-workers, I kept all discussions of the lawsuit limited to my immediate family. Mrs. Collins paused for a moment then continued. "Don't get me wrong. I'm sure that some of them mean well. And I would venture to say that many of them are qualified."

"Right," I agreed. "It's just that somewhere along the way they forget that the children are the real reason that we're here. It has turned into a *quid pro quo* type of relationship in the administration. They keep trying to throw money at the problems when more money is not what is needed. They are not looking at the entire picture, nor are they making the needs of our children a priority. For example, take the busing issue. Look around. The majority of our students are African American. Why are we spending millions of dollars to bus African American students to be with other African American students? There is a school in just about every neighborhood. Why can't the students attend the school in their neighborhood?"

"I didn't realize that busing was that expensive."

"Yes. It's very expensive. Especially when you take into consideration the cost of gas, insurance, and maintenance." I spoke with a passion, trying to communicate the great concern that I felt about this particular subject matter. "It no longer serves the purpose of integration or balancing out the demographics. The white student population only accounts for 4% of the entire student body." I paused and then went on.

"I'm sure eliminating busing would get the community more involved with the schools and take the excuse away from parents of not having transportation to parent meetings. That would be a step in the right direction. As a counselor, one of the biggest issues I face is getting the parents and their community involved in their lives. The parents send their children to the schools without the slightest idea of what's going on regarding their children's education. The people who live in the neighborhoods don't have anything to do with the schools. We need full community involvement. It takes a village to raise a child."

"Exactly." Mrs. Collins nodded strongly in full agreement as I spoke. "That's what our children need. Not to mention the money that it would save. We could use that money to hire more teachers."

"Which would give us smaller classrooms, and Lord knows we need smaller classrooms. I have over 35 students in my homeroom this year. Now you know that's just too many. I keep feeling like I'm stretched too thin. Several of them are two grade levels below in reading and math. I don't have the time or the cooperation of my parents to help them progress. I know they will not receive the skills needed to function successfully in society."

"I can not think of a logical reason why they feel busing is compulsory. But when you really think about it, busing just isn't an efficient or necessary use of funds. There are several benefits that we could get from eradicating busing. It would eliminate the group tardiness that results from the buses running behind schedule and all of the snow days that our students miss. We could also have before and after school activities."

"Yeah, especially tutoring. Over half my students need help with their basic math facts and reading." added Mrs. Collins.

"Let us not forget after school detention, which would really be an ideal replacement for corporal punishment. And last but not least, remove the extra burden that our principals are under as a result of having to deal with bus misconduct."

"Dr. Union, I never thought about it like that. That's a perfect example of what I've been talking about. Honey, you really look at if from all angles.

"Yes, I do. I care about our children, and I try to pay really close attention to what they need. I've been in this system for over 20 years, and I've seen too many of our students leave the system with no hope of qualifying for college or getting a good paying job. Our young men become involved in crime, and our young women end up with three or four children out of wedlock. Then the pattern continues with the next generation. I guess my past work experiences have helped to give me a rounded perspective."

"Well, I'm just so glad that you're here. I know they hated to lose you from your other school, but their loss was definitely our gain. We need someone like you around here. It will be a pleasant change."

"Well, thank you. I'm glad to be here." Feeling a little guilty, I told Mrs. Collins I was glad to be here, but the truth was I wasn't sure of that. I was constantly exploring other options including retiring and even thought about just walking away. Things had gotten to where almost every day was a struggle, although I did feel more at home here since leaving my school of 15 years.

The year that I worked at my previous school, the principal was so impressed with my work that she nominated me for the auspicious Educator of the Year Award, one also given to counselors. Though I was grateful and humbled by the nomination, I never regretted my decision to transfer here. Today's conversation with Mrs. Collins had simply confirmed that I was more than likely in the right place.

My discussion with Mrs. Collins was shared at dinner with Alexander and Roman. When we began talking about the solutions, Roman chimed in with his take on the whole thing. "I just don't think that they take every student into consideration. There is this expectation for every student to go to college, but that is not realistic. Sure I chose the college track, but that may not be for everyone. What about that student who has no plans or just isn't equipped to go to college? Should he or she just fall through the cracks? What kind of self-esteem will such a student have in a system that says you're college-bound or doomed? Not every one wants to go, and not every one will qualify to go. Even some of those who want to go may not be able to afford it. You just never know the cards that life will deal some of the students. Every situation is different."

I looked at Roman, surprised by his commentary, and told him "I actually agree with you. I think there could be far better planning and preparation for those who decide to select a career that does not require four years of college."

"That's what I like about my medical school program. We have those two years in the classroom, and then we do two years of clerkships. It helps to fully prepare us for real world experiences. We get the chance to participate in different specialties so that we'll have a better idea of what we may want to specialize in after we graduate. You'd be surprised how many medical school meltdowns I've heard about. All because some of the schools do not have programs to meet the educational needs of the great diversity in the student body and the real world needs of the students. I think the same goes for students in high school."

"I agree. Our slogan of 'Every Student Will Attend College' is ridiculous. It should be 'Meeting the Needs of Every Child Every Day.' We should offer curricula that will provide our students with skills that they can use after graduating from high school. When our college bound students are handed their diplomas and scholarships, our non-college students should be offered diplomas based on enough skills to allow them to walk directly into a job."

We talked a little more about the school system before the conversation took a gradual turn to the lawsuit. I still hadn't heard back on the appeal, and I was unsure of how to look at the amount of time that it was taking. Was the extended time period a sign that the decision was being heavily considered, or was the process simply bogged down by paperwork, other cases, or an uncooperative school system? Either way, I found myself wondering when I would receive some feedback.

Mrs. Collins often complained about all the tension she felt after leaving school. So, I invited her to come and workout with my group at the fitness center to help relieve some of her job-related stress. I can't say that I expected her to show up, but I was pleasantly surprised when she did. Once we were done, Mrs. Collins and I decided to grab some smoothies. It was obvious that she had something on her mind. I have always felt that teachers are continually placed under a great deal of pressure, and since I was on the same team working towards the same goals, I wanted to be of service. Once we were comfortably seated at The Smoothie Palace, Mrs. Collins began to relax.

"I really enjoyed the class."

"Thanks Mrs. Collins."

"Call me Lucy. I have to admit. You're a different person in there."

"I am. I have a different kind of passion for fitness. I get a natural high during my workout sessions, an endorphin high that has a sort of pain-relieving effect. I find exercise is so refreshing and very rewarding. It allows me to free myself of built up stress that is known to shorten your life span."

"Yeah. I can tell that you really love it. I just don't get how you balance it all-- the fitness center, home, school. Well, it's hard enough to deal with school. I don't expect you to comment on this, but I know that things haven't been perfect at school, either. I just want to know how you keep going. You know that people talk; you come in day in and day out and face these demons every day with a smile. Your work isn't affected, your disposition doesn't seem to be affected, and you're still cordial and warm to both the students and the teachers."

Listening to Lucy talk, I wasn't ready to discuss my lawsuit with anyone in the system, so I definitely wasn't about to touch that topic. It was wiser to learn more by saying nothing and simply lending a listening ear.

"I've been through so much in the 10 years that I've been teaching," Lucy continued. "I never had the courage to face the injustice; instead I spent the last six years running from the skeletons in the closet." By now it had become apparent that I was there in a counseling capacity. She seemed heavily burdened by something, and it seemed that she was just about to share it.

"Don't get me wrong, Dr. Union. I'm happy here at my present school. It's just hard to face those students every day when I know that this system does not have their best interests at heart. There is too much politics going on for these students to get what they need. The corruption runs too deep. Six years ago, I was excited about teaching. I saw this as my chance to mold the minds of tomorrow. I actually bought into the every student every day goes to college hodgepodge"

"What happened six years ago?"

"Him."

"Excuse me?" I wasn't sure if I had heard her right. "Him?"

"I was in my tenure year of teaching working at an elementary school. I'm sure you remember me telling you about my first teaching job. I looked at my principal as my mentor. I was always excited about my one-on-one and any opportunity that I got to pick his brain. I can still remember being confused when his hands started to roam. It started as lingering good-bye hugs. Then it went to gentle pats on the arm. Next thing I know, he was pushing things to the limit. I can recall the exact day when I knew that things had gone too far. I had on a knee length skirt. We were sitting at the table in his office, discussing a few of the behavior issues I was having with my class. He started by touching my hand as he was making a point. Then he worked his way up my arm. I don't know why I didn't stop him then. I can't say that I didn't know where it was going. One minute he's talking to me about my class's standardized test scores, the next minute his hand is up my skirt. He didn't miss a beat. I just sat there and looked straight ahead. I couldn't even look at him. He moaned and breathed hard the whole time. It was so sick. He was such a smart man. He ran the school almost perfectly, but on the other side of that office door, he was sick."

"Oh, Lucy. I am so sorry that you had to go through something like that. It had to be hard to deal with."

"Yeah it was. I remember being so disgusted. Tears formed in my eyes, but I refused to let them run down my cheek. I know he saw the tears; he had to have sensed my anxiety, but he just kept going as if he hadn't noticed my discomfort. I have to admit it. I didn't even say anything. I was too stunned. I didn't say no, or stop it. I just sat there in shock and disgust paralyzed, those tears in my eyes. It must have lasted ten minutes or so. Then he went on with the meeting as if nothing happened.

"You know what's worse? I had to meet with him over and over again until I finally got the position at this school. Sometimes he was straightforward and completely professional. Then other times he went back to his low-down, dirty ways. It made me sick to my stomach to see him interact with other teachers and students, but I never said a word. I was too scared of how it would make me look and that he would not recommend me for a permanent teaching position. I knew there would be people who wouldn't believe me, so I decided not to risk it. He had such an impressive work history and a solid relationship with those in power. I just didn't want to go up against the entire city. I went to work every day with that load on my shoulders. Every time I ran into him, I got nervous. Who knows how many teachers or staff he's done that to? I should have done something about it, but I was just too scared."

"So you've carried this for six years?"

"Yes. My husband doesn't even know. He would kill him. I just wasn't ready to face the fire, so I've kept it to myself."

I listened in shock, unsure of what exactly to say. I wasn't prepared for this type of confession. I was very familiar with the principal she was speaking of. I'd interacted with him several times during my years in the system. Never would I have thought that he was one of the low-lifes. Lucy didn't say much more; rather she sat quietly and sipped her smoothie. While she seemed relieved to have gotten it off her chest, she still seemed burdened by the scars that the offense left. I still didn't speak up about my experience. I just wasn't in a place where I trusted anyone in the system enough to open up about my case.

After my discussion with Mrs. Collins, one-on-one with my new principal took on a whole new meaning. I had a good rapport with Mr. Goodlad. He seemed professional enough, but my degree of trust was somewhat affected. About 30 minutes into the meeting, he took off his glasses and looked me in the eye.

"Dr. Union, I just want you to know that we are glad to have you here. I think it's unfortunate that you've been through so much over the last few years."

"Excuse me?"

"You don't have to confirm nor deny anything. That's not what I'm trying to accomplish right now. I only want to assure you that the rumblings of the grapevine have zero effect on how I view you as an educator. I think the esteem that your last principal held you under is evident. I intend on carrying that forward and building a strong working relationship with you."

"I'm not fully aware of everything that is being said, but I do appreciate having your support as my principal."

"I probably shouldn't be telling you this, but I'm going to level with you. When it became known that you were transferring to my school, I did get a few phone calls about you. The late Mr. Gregory Wallace informed us about your lawsuit. And he assured us that it would not amount to anything. I'm sure Mr. Williams got the same phone calls. I think he and I have different outlooks on things, however. I just want to commend you on a job well done. I also want to assure you that I am here for the students."

"That's good to know."

"I'm interested in my students getting the best possible education that we can give. I'm convinced that we can't do that as long as we play into the politics that the administration sometimes plays. It's hard enough to teach these students with the money being incorrectly allocated and board policy not being followed. My faculty, staff, and I have to concentrate on the business of educating our students. I'm dealing with students, more than half of whom are academically challenged. I need teachers and counselors who are ready to take on that challenge. As far as I'm concerned, we have a lot of work to do. So I'll leave the politics up to the administration."

Unsure of how to process the information that I had just been given, nevertheless, I was very aware of the challenges that the principals and teachers faced on a daily basis. They were charged with teaching students who didn't care much about learning. Many times parental involvement was minimal to none, and the resources were wasted on things that didn't support the overall goal of giving the children the best possible education. I understood his endeavor, but I wasn't sure whether I trusted him enough to speak freely. Therefore, our conversation stayed on a professional level, focused on my mentoring program, and success stories about my students.

We also talked about the oral hygiene program, my career awareness grants and foundation grants. By the time the meeting was over, Mr. Goodlad and I had mulled over several ways to get the students on track and the parents more involved with their child's academic progress. Though I left that meeting feeling hopeful that my students might actually get the education that they deserved, I was still somewhat unnerved by Mr. Goodlad's confirmation of the conspiracy against me.

Alexander heard about my conversation with Mr. Goodlad and didn't seem surprised by it at all.

"Come on baby," Alexander said reasonably. "You already knew that they were going to spread the word about this. That was made clear the first time Williams approached you about declaring you surplus. You knew that Wallace told him about your case and encouraged him to go against you. Did you expect it to stop there?" In fact I would not be surprised if Williams got a little something in exchange for his trouble like his dream school, maybe?

"No not really. It was just weird to actually have it confirmed. It's one thing to suspect you're being talked about. It's another thing to hear it for yourself."

"But you didn't hear it."

"No, but I may as well have. I think he meant well, but he confirmed it all right."

"Yeah. You're right. I just want you to be careful. Goodlad may mean you well and he may be one of the good guys, but I just want you to be sure to keep your guard up. I wouldn't say too much."

"No, I still don't feel comfortable enough to talk to any of them about my case. As a matter of fact, I'd rather keep things between the attorney, you, and me."

"Yeah that's probably best. These days, you just never know whom you can trust. Every body seems to have their own agenda."

"Yeah."

"Don't worry though, baby. You'll have your day soon enough. I can feel it."

I smiled as Alexander reassured me of the peace that was sure to come soon. The road had been long and tough, and I had begun to grow weary. Though each step was purposeful, my feet were long past tired, and my spirit was getting there as well.

With the weight of the pending appeal sitting squarely upon my shoulders, I decided to check in again with Attorney Edelman. I didn't expect to receive anything new, but the anticipation was too much. I had to ask. The conversation with Mary started off as it usually did. "So how are things?" She always asked that first.

"Well, nothing really new." I decided to give her the abbreviated version of my conversation with Mr.Goodlad. "I've gotten off to a decent start at my new school. Every one seems pretty nice, and the needs of the middle students are a lot different from those of the elementary students."

"I bet they are. I'm sure it's a little less stressful."

"A little. My new principal informed me that he did get a couple of phone calls about me before I got there. He all but said that he was told that I would be trouble and that he made a conscious decision not to behave the way they did. He went on to tell me that he did not participate in the politics of the school system and that he respected my work as a counselor."

"Really! We will add him to our list to testify or give a statement on our behalf.

"Yes."

"I'm sure the EEOC would have loved to interview him."

"Yeah right," I answered sarcastically. "Knowing the hold that the school system has on EEOC, regardless, they probably wouldn't have interviewed him anyway. It's clear now that I would have had to walk away from this job completely to get a fresh start. They have put my name all the way through the ringer. I was glad that he was honest with me, but I have to be honest. It was still embarrassing." I went on to share with Mary just how much of an emotional roller coaster everything was for me. One day I was excited about my new school and ready to move forward. The next, I was reliving the embarrassment of being overlooked for job after job and the hurt of the covert putdowns that I experienced.

"Mary, I just need some type of closure. That way I can make a clear decision about where I want to go next in life. Only after this chapter is closed will I be able to begin to write the next chapter of my life. More important than closure, I need some peace."

"Well, I was going to call you this afternoon. But I guess I won't hold you in suspense any longer."

"What?" My heart began to pound. "Call me about what? Hold me in suspense about what?"

"Well, I just got word back about your appeal, and they have made a decision." I listened to her words carefully. I hadn't really expected an update, just a chance to vent to a reliable and confidential source. It seemed, however, that I would get far more than I ever anticipated from that particular phone call.

"You've fought so long and hard, Relia. I really hoped that I would be able to get justice for you."

"Well, I really felt like you were the one for the job."

As I spoke, I wondered if my feelings were right. It seemed that I was only seconds away from finding out.

"Dr. Union, please hold for a just a minute while I take this call", said Mary.

Chapter 9 Highly Qualified?
Does it Matter?

Though the trial lasted only a week or so, the years of waiting on the investigation to be completed and waiting on the trial had made her very existence miserable. By the time the trial came down to the closing arguments, she was beyond ready for some kind of closure. She shifted uncomfortably as the defense attorney gave a venomous closing argument. He took her pride, placed it squarely beneath the sole of his shoe, and stomped out every single fiber of its existence.

Surely it wasn't reasonable doubt that he was trying to create in the minds of the jurors; rather, it was pure disdain. He whispered when he spoke of the years of dedicated service that she gave to the system and raised his voice when he spoke of how she was now betraying them. He raised his voice to just below a shout as he orated about her ultimate intentions to milk the system for a paycheck after she was done, thereby ruining the lives of the defendants. He looked each of the jurors in the eye and asked them to look at the defendants as he read off their résumés. He stressed the difference that each of them had made as educators and the relationships that they shared with their students.

When he was done, the defendants sat with smirks on their faces, strongly confident in the outcome. She, on the other hand, observed the demeanor of each of the jurors. They couldn't look her in the eyes; instead they looked down in confusion and anguish over the decision they were about to be charged with making. She knew that the stage was set for her attackers to walk away with no consequence for their actions. It was imperative that the prosecutor drove home the trauma caused by the invasion she had experienced at the hands of the defendants. However, the evidence was circumstantial at best. Even the investigators didn't seem completely convinced by her account of the attack. She took a deep breath, said a quick prayer, and waited to hear how this whole saga would end.

The prosecutor stood calmly. He adjusted his tie, and then started by clapping sarcastically. "That was certainly an amazingly despicable masterpiece of lies and mischaracterization. It's rather unfortunate that our justice system has resorted to this." The prosecutor's words seemed to liven up the jurors. They raised their heads and instantly became more attentive. All of a sudden his words began to sink in. He connected each circumstantial piece of evidence in a way that painted a very clear picture of the attack. Hope became her life preserver. She gripped her seat tightly enough to redden her knuckles. Once he was done recounting the evidence, he took aim at the character of each of the defendants. Not to be outdone by the defense attorney, he returned the favor and crushed any hopes that the defendants had of walking out of that courtroom unscathed. He reminded the jurors of how one of the defendants, a very popular principal, had been disciplined for carrying on an improper relationship with a teacher. Another defendant, an administrator, who has been accused of "selling promotions" to school employees. He spoke at length about how scandal after scandal had been swept under the rug. "It's despicable that so much of the school system's money has gone to settling sexual harassment and other injustices. And here..." He pointed at the defendants as he raised his voice, "We have a shameful and corrupt representation of the things, or rather people, who are cheating our children out of the education that they deserve."

Not until he finished his closing arguments and was comfortably seated did she breathe. The tension was too high. As if they knew they were doomed, each of the defendants looked over his or her right shoulder and into her eyes. It was obvious that they felt the heat, but even that didn't create remorse. The judge solemnly reminded the jurors of their civic duty. He stressed the importance of decision-making based on the facts and evidence rather than on the emotions dramatized during the trial. They all appeared to be somewhat overwhelmed by the task at hand. They exited to deliberate, heavy with the burden.

"So what do we do now?" She stood next to the prosecutor, unsure of where to go. "We wait." He replied. The nervousness must have showed on her face because his expression softened. He reached out and touched her on the arm. "Look, I know this is difficult for you. This has been going on for so long, and I'm sure you haven't had a good night's sleep since that day."

"Not really."

"Well, I'm not going to lie to you. This could be a really long wait, or it could be a short one. It kind of depends on how emotional the jury is."

"Well the judge just kind of took that away. He was pretty clear about their job. This is about the facts, not about emotion. So there went that."

"Not really. Emotion is natural. It's embedded in us. The jurors who are emotionally driven can't just turn that off. Now, they can try to ignore it, but eventually who they are will prevail and they will end up viewing things from that same emotional perspective. It may be subconscious but it still happens."

"I really hope so. The defense attorney worked really hard to take away any chance of the jury seeing me as a person. I'm the one who had to endure the attack. I had to stare those people in the face. They were the same people that I worked with every day, and I had to lay there as they raped me. How I am not supposed to be emotional? How am I supposed to go to work every day? How am I supposed to go on?"

The prosecutor stood speechless, unsure of how to comfort her very valid concerns. He had no answers for her. She knew this and walked out of the courthouse and down the steps without looking back. She couldn't look back. In her mind, she had far too much in front of her to figure out. The damage had been done. She needed to figure out how to move on.

CHAPTER 9

"I am so sorry for that interruption," said Attorney Edelman. "I was trying to let you know that the Court of Appeals reversed the summary judgment!"

It took at least five minutes for any feeling to return to my legs. I knew the literal meaning of each of the words that Attorney Edelman spoke, but thought I had to have misunderstood what they meant when lumped together into one sentence. The understanding froze my speech because it all just seemed too good to be true.

"Hello? Are you still there?" Attorney Edelman spoke in a kidding voice. "I expected a big reaction, but I don't know if I expected it to be this big. Don't get me wrong. I thought you would be speechless, but not speech-less."

"Yes. I've been waiting for a long time to hear this, but I'm not sure if I really believed that I would ever actually hear it. One day, I'm out there fighting to be heard and taken seriously; years later, I'm being vindicated. Finally, justice."

"I'm not so sure that I would go so far as to call it justice--just yet. We still have to reach a settlement."

"What do you mean? They don't have a choice but to settle now, right?"

"Well, yes! It has been declared, in fact, that this was a case of racial discrimination, and now they will more than likely have to pay. The question is, how much? I'm sure you have your own ideas of what it was worth to you, but chances are they have a completely different idea of what it's worth. Now I will say this, we did win the toughest battle, but the war is not over yet."

"Okay, well, what's next?"

"Well, there are a couple of ways that this can end. We can try to reach a settlement. If that doesn't work, then we can have what's called an alternative dispute resolution. That's just a meeting between them and us. At this meeting, we'll mediate, and a decision is made then. If all else fails and push comes to shove, we'll have to go to trial."

"Oh, so this really isn't over yet?"

"Not yet, but at least the standard has been set. We just have to drive this thing on home."

"I just can't believe that they reversed the judge's decision."

"Well, I'm going to give the whole decision a closer look. Depending on the precedents that they used to come up with the decision, I can try to figure out our next move. I know you can't wait to share the news with your husband. I'm sure he'll be excited as well. I'll let you go and just give you a call in a couple of days."

It was tough to contain my excitement as I made the trip home. I pondered the idea of calling Alexander and sharing the news with him over the phone. Instead, I decided to share it with the whole family face to face. As tough as it was, I made the entire ride home without picking up the phone and calling Alexander. This in itself was a challenge for me!

Just as I intended, I arrived at the house some time before Alexander. When I called, he informed me that it would be at least another hour before he made it home. So, I had the perfect opportunity to prepare a quick but elegantly celebratory dinner. Both Roman and Addison had accepted my invitation to join us for a special dinner. Though they knew I had an announcement of some kind, they were still in the dark about what it concerned.

Just over an hour later, we were all settle, and three sets of eyes, full of curiosity, focused on me. They'd take a bite, then stare at me, look around, and then take another bite. I kind of enjoyed watching them squirm, and made it a point to appear to be enjoying my dinner a little more than I actually was. Finally, the suspense became too much for Addison, and he decided to take the reins.

"Okay, so the food is really great and all, but you know you didn't invite us over here just to eat. Don't get me wrong. It's really great spending quality time with you all. But you're killing me."

"Pardon me." I joked with Addison. "I don't know what you're talking about."

"Come on Mom!" Roman and Addison repeated in unison several times. "What is it?"

"Okay, okay." I finally gave in and decided to put them out of their misery. I put the fork down, pushed my plate back, and blurted the good news out. "We won the appeal. The decision was reversed!"

"What?" Addison inquired with a huge smile on his face. "Was it time to hear back already?"

"I didn't think so, but I called to ask Mary today for an update, just like I'd done every other week. She actually let me go on for a few minutes before she told me."

"So, it's really happening," Roman seemed pleasantly stunned. "I mean, we all knew that you deserved it, and that they would eventually have to pay.

"Mom, you preserved and believed in God's word: 'All things are possible.' Luke 18:27." It's just surreal that you're that much closer to your victory. By the way, how close are you?"

"Yeah Mom, what's next?"

"Well, we are looking into a couple of options. One is to try to reach a settlement. If we can't, we can have meetings with them and a mediator who would help us reach an agreement. The other option is a trial, where a jury or a judge would decide the outcome."

"So what are you leaning towards?" Roman was naturally inquisitive. The same curiosity that makes him perfect for the medical field caused him to ask questions, sometimes more quickly than they could be answered. "I'm not sure Roman; the attorney is weighing the options. She has to read the entire decision carefully before deciding the best way to proceed."

"How long before she'll decide?"

"She said that she's going to give me a call in a couple of days. We'll still need to sit down and mull it over."

"Dad," Addison continued. "You should make sure to go to that meeting."

"Roman is right, Dad. The next move needs to be carefully planned. That school system has so many people in its pockets. I'm not sure if you could get a fair shot using a judge or a jury either for that matter." Alexander seemed to be in his own little world. "Dad? Hey, you're mighty quiet over there. What are you thinking about?" There was a short pause before he answered. "Oh don't pay me any attention. I'm just sitting here thinking about how amazing your mother really is." He turned his gaze to me. "Relia baby," Alexander's eyes locked in on mine. "I can't tell you just how proud of you I am. You hung in there and kept it together. I know it isn't over, but I have a feeling that you can handle just about anything that they can possibly throw your way now. You've proven that you have what it takes to fight this thing to the end. Dr. Relia Union, you are quite a woman."

The silence at the table was comfortable. I looked across the table at my hero and felt every single familiar butterfly flutter in my stomach. He'd given me the kind of life and marriage that some women only dreamed about. Here he was looking at me with the same twinkle that caused me to marry him long before many of my family and friends thought we were ready. There he sat with eyes as sure as tomorrow, radiating sheer admiration. Our love was indeed for the big screen, as normal life simply couldn't contain it.

"Okay, we get it. You're in love. That's really great, but I have another question though."

"You know what Roman...," I interrupted abruptly and allowed the boys to rejoin us on planet earth. I gave Alexander the "to be continued" look, before turning my attention back to Roman. "For some reason, that doesn't surprise me."

"So have you thought about what's next for you, career wise? Do you think you can continue to work in that school system after going through all of this?" Once again, my son had posed the million-dollar question.

"Probably not, Roman, but I think we should try to hold off on thinking about that for now. Let's enjoy this moment and take it all in. Also, I have to stay focused on seeing this through to the end. We can't afford to take our eyes off the finish line".

"Justice is finally within reach." Alexander proclaimed.

Alexander was right. Justice did seem to be in reach, but it was still hard to fully believe that it was actually attainable. I couldn't help but think about all I'd seen and experienced over the last 25 years. Before applying for my first teaching job, I was told how things worked in the school system by a graduate school classmate who had very influential connections. "Getting your degree is one thing," she said, "but it's really about who you know. My job is already lined up. My mother is kinda seeing one of the big suits. He's married and high on the food chain, so I won't say his name, but he lined it up for me. Look Relia, you have your degree and everything, but I'm afraid that's just not going to get it. It's all about who you know."

It should have been apparent then that my career would run across a bump or two. From day one the signs were there, and it was obvious that a certain payoff came with having connections. I had truly believed however, that my skills, compassion, and dedication to the students would smooth out that road for me. I felt I could adapt to the cliques; even the instances of gender-based harassment soon became easy to overlook. However, never did I expect the racial discrimination. The school system boasted an African American student population of 90% and an employee population of 88% African American. Statistically speaking, it seemed very unlikely that an African American woman like me would experience what the past several years had brought my way.

It is hard to forget the cold stares that greeted me during my first interview. The line of questioning was investigative rather than explorative. Just thinking of that day and how belittling they had been caused a twinge of anger to creep into my spirit. Before long, peace evaded me and I found myself up at a very familiar dark and lonely time of night. Since there had been enough turmoil for the night, I plopped down on the sofa in exhaustion.

There was a crunch from a magazine that I pulled from beneath my bottom. As if it were sent directly from God, it gave me a marvelous sign of hope. It was the inaugural issue of *Ladies Magazine,* and I instantly remembered that I would be featured. I flipped to the article and looked at my picture. My disposition at work was a far cry from the lively passionate woman who was all but jumping off the pages of this article, and I wondered why that confidence always seemed to disappear immediately after stepping foot into the school hallways. The freedom and happiness that came from changing the lives of women through fitness, no longer carried over into my educational career.

Just as she promised, Attorney Edelman called me a few days later to discuss the next steps. This excitement was short lived, when she let me in on a piece of not so good news. "I have some good news and some not-so good news."

"Okay, I think I'll take the bad first."

"I was reading over the full decision from the Court of Appeals, and they have pretty much laid out the basis of our case. They did affirm the judge's decision on the racial discrimination, but not the retaliation."

"Wait, what do you mean they affirmed the judge's decision?"

"Well, the Court of Appeals overturned the retaliation ruling, but they affirmed the racial discrimination ruling."

"What does that mean for me?"

"That means that we're still alive on the discrimination claim, but we may be out of steam on the retaliation claim. Most of the precedents had stronger examples. Maybe the courts just didn't feel like there was sufficient causation to reverse the judge's decision."

"But that's the biggest part of it. Yeah, the discriminatory hiring practices are one thing. However, the major issue is not what they did that moment but how they erased my ability to maximize my potential. I was terminated from the school after giving over a decade of excellent service, after which they refused to allow me to interview for over 14 other positions. These were positions that I knew were well within my skill set and qualifications, but they overlooked me time and time again. There is no reason that I shouldn't be doing something other than counseling. What about the embarrassment and shame that I went through? My name has become mud. Even today, years later, I'm still looking over my shoulder wondering when they are going to pull another stunt. If all the mess that's happened over these years isn't sufficient causation, then someone needs to tell me what is."

"Well, I'm sure we can still leverage some of the downstream affects of the retaliation, so don't get too caught up on that part. I'm going to do my best to make them pay for it. We have enough to get them to the table, and that's all we really needed. We got a foot in the door, now we just have to try to bust it wide open. Don't worry; I'm devoted to making sure that you get the justice that you deserve. Besides, we didn't come this far for nothing, right? "

"You're right! You've been so supportive through this process. I believe in you enough to know that I can relax and let you do your thing. So what's next?"

"Well, their attorney contacted me, and it looks like they are ready to meet with us."

"They contacted you? Really? They refused to talk this entire time, and now all of a sudden they're contacting us to meet. That has to be a good thing."

"Yes it is. After the summary judgment was reversed, they figured it would be in everyone's best interest to meet. So it looks like we'll be going with mediation. It shows that they recognize that we have some power, too. It's definitely obvious that they are taking this thing a lot more seriously now."

"Mediation. I'm not sure about that. That means my judgment will rest with one judge. This is the school system we're talking about here; they have their hands in everything, so what if we get a biased judge?"

"We'll face that same dilemma with a jury too. So either way we go, that is a possibility. I don't know if it makes you feel any better, but judges are usually more knowledgeable about the legal aspects of the case and can usually better gauge the severity of the actions involved; on the other hand, a jury may look at things and say 'no big deal.'"

"The biggest thing that we want to consider is the time factor. This has already been going on long enough. If we take this to trial we're looking at as much as another year or so before we get a trial date. If we win the trial, they can appeal that and drag it out another few years. It could take as much as five years before we'd ever see a resolution, let alone a check. Now, ultimately the decision is yours, but I think it's pretty safe to say that we both want a speedy and fair resolution to this. Just think about it."

I decided to go with my attorney's gut instinct on this one. Besides, she was the sole reason that we had gotten this far. She went to bat for me and had given my case everything she had. She could have given up when we received the initial summary judgment, but Mary believed in me and my case. I had every reason to believe that she would bring this thing home.

My attorney immediately went to work on preparing for the mediation. In the meantime, I continued to get acquainted with my new students and colleagues. My future in the school system was up in the air each day. I kept in mind that the outcome of mediation could also deeply affect my future career plans. As tough as it may have been, I was determined not to make any final decisions until after mediation. I would, in the meantime, work as diligently and as passionately as ever.

Sometime before receiving the decision from the Court of Appeals, I had begun working on a Black History Knowledge Bowl for the students. In getting acquainted with my new colleagues and students, I soon realized that student confidence was one of the things that was missing. To help build their confidence and promote self-esteem, I came up with the Black History Knowledge Bowl idea. This would allow the students to learn that people like themselves were able to accomplish great things regardless of the negative circumstances while simultaneously engaging in some friendly competition against other students on their grade level. I gave their teachers study guides in an attempt to level the playing field. It was amazing to walk by classrooms and hear the students preparing for the

Knowledge Bowl. The excitement was high, and they seemed to be having a lot of fun learning.

Their excitement made me want to make sure that the event would be a major success. I wanted it to be a day of change for some students and a day full of wonderful memories for others. I began to pump up the bowl--spreading the word through newsletters, flyers, and word of mouth. The parents of every student as well as the board members received invitations to the event. This allowed us to showcase all of the hard work that the students put into preparing for the bowl.

Thankfully, the principal and teachers all seemed to be equally excited about seeing our students shine. After three weeks of hard work, the day was upon us. The gym was transformed into a mock television game show set. My principal allowed me to purchase professional game show buzzers and extra large trophies to add to the excitement. Much to my surprise, the parents and invited guests began to file into the gym, cameras and balloons in hand. For those students who didn't have parents there, we had faculty and staff yelling and cheering for them with all of their might. Mr. Goodlad had purchased prizes for each participant. It was amazing! The students all showed up dressed in their Sunday best with enthusiastic grins on their faces. As if the questions were no match for their great minds, the students breezed through level after level until finally we had winning teams. No team went unrewarded, and by the end of the awards ceremony, camera flashes filled the air as eager parents took photos of their children with medals, trophies, and certificates. The grand prize trophy was taller than most of the students. Mrs. Collins beamed with pride as her class stood around the trophy and posed happily for the picture that would later be featured in the district's newspaper.

It seemed small at the time, but something happened that day. I realized a few things about our students and even more about this system that just wasn't getting the job done for them. It wasn't that the students were hopelessly lost; we were. They had the brain capacity and ability to learn anything. They just weren't being properly motivated or given the tools that they needed to be successful. The administration was full of people who were not truly qualified to run a household, let alone a school system. Those who were qualified were too busy beating down the teachers and ensuring their own job security to see that we were failing our students.

The parents also played a major part in the success of the Black History Knowledge Bowl. The students felt important for at least those few hours, and they seemed to step up and shine for that reason. This was outstanding because most of our previous events had extremely low parental involvement.

In hindsight, I realize that was the day when I began to seriously ponder my future in the school system. Things were not changing and as a counselor with a sincere interest in providing the best possible education experience for every student, I no longer felt like I belonged. It was as if no-one was driving the bus, and we were all just riding and hanging on for dear life. I needed an environment where the odds weren't against me. I longed for a career where I could give passionately and not wonder where my efforts were going. I no longer wanted to be in a place where vengeance and spitefulness has room to breathe and fester.

After each conversation with Lucy Collins, a teacher who wanted nothing more than to mold the minds of tomorrow, a small piece of me left the building. She still carried around the weight of being violated by someone she looked up to as a mentor. We were one and the same, both violated and left shamefully exposed. While her shame was physical, I really was unable to separate that from my own feeling of shame. Though it wasn't official and there still was a lot to think about, my outlook had changed a great deal. The Relia Union who once served with passion had been transformed and scarred by what the school system had done. Chances were the damage had been done, and it was time to start anew.

Conclusion

The first step out of the doors of the courthouse brought a barrage of reporters. Not until that moment did she realize just how much attention her case had received. The constant flashes of the cameras made the setting even more surreal. Questions were flying through the air quicker than she could comprehend them. She still hadn't gotten the chance to let it all sink in. One moment she was fighting for justice, next she was standing all alone watching the results of her perseverance. The podium was still several feet away, but already the spotlight was on her.

"So how do you feel about the verdict?"

"What are your future career plans? Will you continue to work as a teacher?"

"How do you feel about the fact that some of your attackers are still working?"

The reporters were relentless. They surrounded her in a tight circle, unwilling to give her a chance to breathe. She wanted to answer their questions, but the words just wouldn't come out. The attention of the reporters shifted momentarily as they rushed to try to get comments from the family and loved ones of her attackers. None of them commented; instead they stared with viciousness at her. The silent confrontation lasted for a few seconds before the families continued the short walk back to their respective vehicles.

The short distraction gave her just enough time to gather her thoughts, and when the reporters rushed back her way, she was ready to give her plight a voice. The first question couldn't have been more perfect. "How do you feel about today's verdict?"

"I'm sure that some would say that I should be elated about a guilty verdict. I'm sure that some would say that a certain peace should come with knowing that my attackers will be punished for their crimes. Now, please don't get me wrong. I am satisfied with the outcome of the trial. I just can't say that I'm ecstatic. I can't find total peace in it, and I am still overcome with uneasiness.

"I've spent my life committed to educating our children. The classroom was my sanctuary for change. I was fully devoted to ensuring that our children had a fighting chance at becoming successful adults. When this attack happened, my passion lessened. The classroom became tainted, and my students lost their top spot on my list of priorities. Protecting myself and defending my own honor became more important. For every minute that we spent concentrating on this, a minute was taken away from our children. For every hour that I spent reliving this whole nightmare, an hour of instructional and learning time was taken away from one of my students. So while I'm comforted to know that these people will be punished, I hate that it may have come at the expense of our children."

"Do you plan to return to your job as a teacher?"

"As I stated earlier, the classroom has always served as my sanctuary; the students were my hope." She paused as a knot rose up in her throat. She fought the tears and continued, *"Things are not the same. I'm not sure that they will ever be the same. That classroom has been polluted, but the children continue to be my hope. With that being said, I am unable to return to the classroom at this time. I believe that every educator should do so with passion. If the passion dies, so does their purpose. My passion has shifted, as has my purpose. I am taking a leave of absence from teaching effective immediately."*

"Is there anything else that you would like people to know about you or what you have been through?" She thought about the question for just a second before smiling and answering. *"Yes. Even with all that I've been through, I still believe in the School System in general. I firmly believe that it is filled with teachers who are highly proficient and who*

care more about the students than they do about themselves. I can attest to the effort that they give every day. We have a system that affords our children the opportunity to be more than they could ever dream. However, just as every system, family, or person has its flaws, so does our school system. But just as we do not deserve to be judged by our imperfections, we should not judge it by its imperfections.

I want to say thank you to every teacher who gave me a reassuring nod, who stayed with me through long grueling planning sessions, to those who worked with me, and even those who were too afraid to stand by me. I believe in you, I appreciate you, and even more so, I commend you."

CONCLUSION

Tension hung over the room in a cloud thick enough to suffocate us all. My attorney and I sat on one side of the conference room table as the attorneys for the system sat across from us. The exchange between the attorneys was full of legal jargon, but it didn't all fly over my head. Even as we sat at the table, there was still no admittance of wrongdoing. Every time Mary approached the topic of retaliation, they shut her down.

"I'd like to remind both parties that we are only here to discuss the discrimination charges," the mediator stated clearly. "There was summary judgment in regards to the retaliation charges. That decision was upheld by the Court of Appeals; therefore, we will not consider it in this discussion." The mediator was stern in his warnings. Mary didn't seem the least bit disheartened as she continued to press forward on my behalf. She balanced on the line that separated discrimination and retaliation, hoping that it would blur in the eyes of justice. I cringed every time that a clear distinction was made between the two. If only they had walked in my shoes. They would have realized that the assault did not stop the moment that Amy Folder was awarded the position. That, in fact, it was only the tip of the iceberg. The retaliation was the salt in the wounds. The pain came with me unfairly losing a position that I'd spent over 20 years building; that is when things became unbearable. They did not seem willing to consider what I experienced as the pariah of the system. No one seemed to find it the least bit odd that I was never allowed to interview for positions after I filed the EEOC claim. No matter how they tried to justify, I still found their position deplorable.

The mediation lasted almost the entire day. We went over every line of the briefs as each attorney weighed in on the facts. The mediator seemed unmoved by either side. Finally, after seven hours of being shut up in the conference room, we seemed to reach an impasse. The system felt that it was in their best interest to resolve the discrimination case, but the burden of the weight fell on the retaliation portion. Without it, the board felt no obligation to consider the long-term impacts of their actions. The discussion slowed, and everything that I'd been through took the form of a dollar amount, which Mary presented.

"Okay so if you'll just sign right here, it'll be over. All those years of dealing with this, and it comes down to your signature. I know that it couldn't have been easy. I mean, it was hard for me, and I'm certainly not the one whom it happened to. I can't imagine what these past seven years have been like for you. Anyway, I'm just glad we were able to get what was due to you." I watched her lips move. I wanted to scream, "What was due?" I opened my mouth to protest, but found no words.

"I mean do you know how many people have been wronged by an employer?" Mary spoke softly and logically. "This was a major accomplishment on your part, and I'm so glad that I was able to be a part of it."

"Maybe you're right. I should just take it, huh?"

"I think so. But in the end, it's your choice."

"I just can't believe that all of those years come down to this. I sacrificed a lot to pursue justice, and I'm just not sure how to feel now that I'm looking at what it should be worth on paper."

I shook as I took the settlement offer into my hands and lifted the pen to sign it. I always thought that having judgment in my favor would automatically heal the residual wounds. Now as I digested the dollar amount that some random decider of justice had assigned to my pain, I was certain that this would in no way lead to my healing. It wasn't just about me. It was about the duty that I felt that I owed society to ensure that the injustice would stop here, and that no child would lose a piece of himself in the corrupt hole of a system that we call education. I lifted the pen and attempted to sign, but my hand didn't move.

"Can I have a few more minutes to think about this?"

"Sure. I'm going to step out for a minute. Just come and get me when you're ready." I sat still and gazed at the agreement. It symbolized so much more than a check for my trouble. This symbolized a journey, a purpose, and justice. Before I realized what I was doing, I had Alexander on the phone for his advice. "I knew this day would come. I just didn't think it would be this hard. I truly believed that we would meet, agree on a number, I'd sign it, and go on with my life."

"But what?"

"But I have the agreement in front of me, and I still feel this huge obligation to get it right."

"Get what right, baby? You already got it right. You love those kids. You have changed the lives of thousands of children. You have fought a very unpopular and lonely fight for justice. You are a wonderfully supportive wife and mother. Baby, there is no way that you could get this wrong. The dollar amount doesn't matter; it's your perseverance that counts."

"I know. I'm not saying that it should be about the money, I just-"

"Relia, we're doing just fine financially. Let's be honest. Money is not high on our list of worries. That's exactly why I don't want you to get too concerned about the figure. Just remember: There is no way that you can walk away from this as anything less than a winner."

"I don't know why, but I still feel some anxiety about signing this."

"What did your attorney say?"

"She thinks we're in a good place. She said considering the fact that we don't have the retaliation to consider, and the time that we've spent on this, this seems like a pretty solid deal."

"Well, I really have to agree that this has been a long hard fight. The thing to consider is whether you've accomplished your goal and whether you think you've impacted how future generations will be treated. If you have, then it's okay to close this chapter and move forward. If you haven't, let's figure out the next move and keep it going."

Suddenly everything was back in perspective. After hanging up with Alexander, I took some time and considered what he had mentioned. I realized that for some, their outlook on the school system would have been forever compromised. However, my opinion of the school system that wronged me was contrary to that. I still felt that the children had the benefits of a very respected and well-resourced educational system at their fingertips. The system had the ability to meet every need of every student from a mental, academic, social, and physical standpoint. It also offered everything that the children required to succeed. The teachers worked diligently, each day as proof of their dedication to their students.

No, my opinion of the school system was far from compromised. I sat here as an opponent of a few people who, somewhere along the way, lost sight of what was important. They were the issue. This whole fight was about showing them that it wasn't okay to make decisions based on their own social preferences, but that the needs of our children should always be top priority. Considering that, I felt vindicated. I felt that somehow I'd made at least a little difference in how my successors would be treated.

When Mary poked her head back into the conference room, I motioned her to enter. "So; are we set to go?"

"Yes." I answered, now radiating the confidence that was missing only moments ago. "I'm ready."

"Are you sure? As your attorney, I'm here to advise you, but ultimately the decision is yours. I want you to be completely comfortable with your decision. There's no rush."

"Oh. I'm comfortable with it." I paused and made eye contact with her. "I don't know if I can ever really thank you enough. We must have talked to over fifty different attorneys. No one was brave enough to take on the school system. We searched high and low, looking for just one person to stand up for us. Then we met you. We dropped this case in your lap a day before the filing deadline and you reacted fast, professionally. You could have given up on us, but you didn't."

"As I told you then, I really believed in your position. There is no way I would've sat this one out. It was just too important. Besides," Mary spoke with a joking smile, "You and your husband were a big help by staying on top of things and constantly providing me with valuable documentation."

I signed the agreement and slid it across the table to Mary.

"So, do you see her often?"

"Who," I asked knowing all too well whom she was referring to. "You mean Amy?"

"Yes, now that she has returned to her director position. She only spent one year as a principal, so apparently they did not fill her former director position, and she was allowed to return with no questions asked. I was told that her lack of classroom experience caused her major problems in trying to operate a school. There was a time when I had a twinge of anger, a bit of resentment, and large doses of disappointment every time I listened to her speak. She reeked of inexperience, and an invalidated sense of entitlement. She didn't deserve the position, and the students certainly deserved more."

"I'm sure it's tough."

"It was for a while, but I've gotten over it. I can't really blame her. She didn't hire herself; she probably doesn't even know that she wasn't qualified. It doesn't matter though. I'll be retiring this year. I think I've done my part." Mary nodded in agreement. "Relia, I have to admit it. You're a trooper. You really have done your part. I admire you. This case has been refreshing. I'm just glad that I could be a small part of it all."

Over the seven years, Mary and I had become friends of a sort, bound by a mutual accomplishment. We paused for a moment to take in the finality of it, before saying our good-byes.

In the years leading up to the settlement, I found the nights to be the toughest times of the day. Sure, I faced each new school day with dread, but at least they had the glimmer of hope that the students brought. The nights however, were abysmal. The darkness served as the perfect backdrop for the memories that replayed in my mind over and over again. I replayed moments of foolish security that I often experienced among my peers. I relived the interviews that were actually nothing more than staged sessions of interrogation, aimed at assassinating my self-esteem. Every night I watched a new episode of my life, each one attacking my ability to fully move forward.

Some nights, Alexander sat awake with me, trying desperately to ease a pain that even he couldn't soothe. Other nights I sat alone and faced each urge, every twinge, and countless tears in solitude. Never in a million years would I have imagined that a violation in my professional life could spill so far over into my personal life. I'd always lived a private life that consisted of little more than my family. However, dealing with the betrayal caused me to pull in even tighter. I found myself ignoring the phone calls of friends and loved ones. I even shied away from conversations and social settings that I would have normally welcomed. The effort that it took to sound normal was more than I could afford to give. So the nights served as both my enemy and my refuge. They sheltered me from the burden of having to pretend, but at the same time served as a daunting reminder of just how cruel the world could be.

So, with apprehension, just a few hours after signing the settlement agreement, I watched the night fall. I waited on the familiar gloom to come down and the episodes to replay. Instead, fatigue set in. That night, I rested soundly. For the first time in years, I enjoyed a peaceful night's sleep. With the lawsuit now in the past and a new future to look forward to, I looked foremost to reintroducing myself to the nights. I sought to transform the gloom that usually came with nightfall into a hope that could accompany every sunset. For each one offered a new chance to change a life, to start again, to build on progress.

My Concerns
and
Suggested Solutions

Introduction to Concerns and Solutions Regarding Our Educational System

My concerns stem from the deterioration and failure educational system caused by lack of money and ineffective teachers. Even though the majority of our politicians believe that the answer to our educational system's problems is more money and more training, paperwork, responsibility, and accountability for our teachers, the following points will show that poor teachers and lack of money are not the problem.

In my experience, the majority of our teachers are very sincere, supportive, caring and competent; furthermore, they went above and beyond the call of duty. In fact, most of their frustrations were caused by time wasted on required non-instructional activities and decisions made by board members that were detrimental to the education of students.

I fully agree with Neal Smatresk's statement (president of University of Nevada, Las Vegas, UNLV) "It's not about blaming teachers, it's about revealing the problems we have and then honestly developing strategies to resolve them." Apparently, the Nevada School System discovered that more than a third of high school graduates who enrolled at the state's universities and colleges required remedial classes in English and Mathematics (Richmond, 2009). Moreover, Ruben Murillo, president of the Clark County Education Association, said that students arrive at school with a host of challenges, many of which cannot be solved by even the best of classroom instruction. Murillo further states that when assessing students for readiness for college, some component should deal with their home life and any lack of family support (Richmond, 2009). Julie Greenberg, senior policy director for the National Council on Teacher Quality, a Washington, D.C. based advocacy group, stated, "You can have a fantastic teacher doing a perfectly competent job, but the kids are still below grade level. There's a lot of confounding variables (Richmond, 2009)."

As stated previously, students bring many issues to the classroom, and this is why I find it hard to comprehend how the blame for our failing system can be placed on one group of people, our teachers. For example, Michelle Rhee, the newly appointed Chancellor of Washington, is photographed with a broom on the cover of Time Magazine, December 2008 issue. Her answer to the problem is to get rid of ineffective teachers and to take away teachers' tenure. Her background consists of three years of teaching and running a non-profit business that helps schools recruit good teachers. She is a Korean American raised in a family that placed a high value on education (Ripley, 2008). Placing a high value on education is a historical trend among Korean and Southeast Asian families. As a group, Asian Americans have done better academically than other cultural minority groups in the American educational system (Lee, 1997). In fact, they are often referred to as the model minority. They usually score higher on achievement tests, and a higher percentage of them complete college compared to students of all other races (National Center Education Statistics, 2005). The parents of these children, as Rhee's parents did, usually have high expectations for their children and encourage them not only to attend college but also to attain graduate degrees (Okagaki & Frensch, 1998). The study of Huntsinger, Jose, & Larsen found that these parents were ten times more likely to provide school-related practice activities at home for their preschoolers and kindergarten children than other races (1998). Given Ms. Rhee's belief that getting rid of the ineffective teachers is the answer, I wonder if she did not study the culture of the families that she is serving. A study done by Berndt shows the value of education is much lower in some cases for most minorities (1999). In such cultures, academic success is viewed as "selling out", and often, African American role models are not connected to academic success. They usually represent the music industry and are seen as being tough and cool. In my experience, my students were told by their parents to do "bad" on educational psychological assessments so they could qualify for special educational services. Such parents receive extra money for those students who qualify for special education. For example, during a meeting with one parent, I had a father boast about having four children in special education, and after this meeting, he said, "Now I will have a fifth child placed in special ed." Bill Cosby stated during the Annual Rainbow/PUSH Conference May 17, 2004 at a NAACP dinner in Washington, D.C., "The lower economic people are not holding up their end in this deal. These people are not parenting; they are buying things for their kids…$500.00 sneakers for what? But they won't spend $200 for Hooked on Phonics" (2009). My experience mirrors Mr. Cosby's statement. My students who are without the basic school supplies (pencils and paper) on a regular basis are the same students who bring large sums of money to attend our Mid-South Fair. Their parents tend to have lower aspirations and allow their children to fall between the cracks. Several of my friends and co-workers removed their children from public schools because of the lack of focus on education. One of my friends' sons shared with her that, "I want to go to a school where other kids have the same goals as I do." My oldest son requested to leave his middle school because he stated that his friend was "jumped on" in the bathroom because he "answered too many questions." One of my co-workers removed her children from public school because the focus was on disruptive behavior rather than academic achievement. The majority of my counseling time was spent working with students who demonstrated inappropriate behavior, which usually led to poor academic performance or vice versa. These were the same students whose parents were difficult to contact and who had no involvement in their children's school life. However, my youngest son attended a public optional school (college preparatory) where learning was the main focus. At this school, we experienced 99.9% parental involvement. The principal was empowered strictly to enforce the restrictions and requirements for behavior and grades.

My understanding of the No Child Left Behind Act is the focus is on accountability for students (which is determined by high-stakes testing), teachers, and principals. The once shared responsibility among parents, administrators, and teachers for our children's academic achievement is no longer emphasized according to the new national educational trend (Christenson, 2004). I failed to read in the No Child Left Behind Act where parents and board members, those who make the decisions about students, teachers, and principals, were held accountable for erroneous decisions.

Those who have the authority to make changes in our educational system must have the insight to see that without parental involvement, little improvement if any will be made. President and Mrs. Obama support this fact first by serving as role models and second by continually emphasizing that parental involvement is necessary if our children are to succeed.

Our country spends more per pupil on early childhood programs through high school than most developed nations. However, our students can not compete with children of other such nations in the basic subjects (Ripley, 2008). Our school system has everything that any child could possibly need to work up to his or her potential; specifically, we have services that provide for children's physical, social, academic, nutritional, and emotional needs. Consider Section 504 Plan of the Rehabilitation Act of 1973, which, "requires recipients (school systems) to provide to students with disabilities appropriate educational services designed to meet the individual needs of such students to the same extent as the needs of students without disabilities are met" (U.S. Department of Education, Office for Civil Rights, 2009). This act assisted me in getting home-bound teachers for students who became pregnant and supplying needy students with laptop computers. One special education student who was emotionally disturbed could not spend the entire day at school, so his special educational team decided that it was in his best interest to leave after lunch. Therefore, this student and only this student was picked up daily and delivered to his home by a school bus. A parent who can not attend a meeting or take that child to a doctor's appointment due to lack of transportation will be picked up and taken to his or her destination by the school's parent advocate. If a parent disagrees with the results of psychological testing done by our school system, the school system will pay a private agency to retest the student. The system feeds the students two to three times a day and provides clothing if necessary. Vision and hearing screenings are done periodically. Accommodations are made for those students needing speech therapy or physical therapy. Students with behavior problems can have a behavior specialist (one-on-one) assigned to them on an all-day daily basis. Students who are experiencing severe emotional problems are assigned to small classes (6-7 students). The students' individual educational plans can be carried out by a certified special education teacher who will have as many as three special education teacher assistants. In some cases, a student will have a certified special education teacher and a teacher assistant assigned specifically to him/her within a small classroom setting (Individual with Disabilities Education Act of 1997, 2004). These services are in place and being utilized.

Unfortunately, most of the money available for our students usually does not make it to the correct destination. So much of the taxpayer's hard earned money is simply wasted. I repeat it is simply wasted, and yet the budget of some school systems is almost twice the budget of our city (Vergos, 2007).

In the pages that follow, I will attempt to explain what I interpret as the major problems facing our children, our city and our nation and the solutions for these many problems. I will be drawing from experiences and observations that I have obtained from spending thousands of hours in several different schools. This will include my daily contacts with thousands of teachers, students, parents, administrators, school psychologists, social workers, case workers, and a variety of resource people. I accumulated this information while I was a teacher, an elementary counselor, a middle school counselor, an acting principal and an acting counseling director.

We are a proud Nation that boasts of our vast human resource, but we are quickly losing ground. Nationwide, our students are not working up to their potential, and they show no interest in trying to reach academic goals that will lead them into the job market. Also, some parents do not have high expectations for their children, and some of our high-ranking school administrators do not have the knowledge base or interest in our students that is so badly needed. In these ways, we are allowing our human resources to deplete, and therefore, I am very concerned. My concern has led me to do research and formulate solutions. Ultimately, my greatest concern is for my home town where I was born and raised and chose to raise my family and start a career. I love my home, but I believe it is being infiltrated by ignorance. I mean no harm or disrespect to anyone. But you can only solve a problem when it is realized and then owned. These facts must be shared for you to realize and take ownership of them so that the future of our children and our great city will be able to receive the much needed change and positive development. By no means does my home town stand alone in regards to this horrible situation. Nevertheless, many school systems across our nation face these same problems. Please take the time to read about some of the factors that worry me and the strategies that could possibly help solve these problems in all school systems. And they just might spark an idea in your line of thinking.

As I invite you to look for ways to improve any growing educational system faced with an overload of problems once the children hit the front door, please consider each of the following questions.

What responsibility does a parent have regarding his/her child's education?

Parents play a crucial part in the education of their children in having the greatest influence, in being the first role models, and in inculcating morals and values, which in turn are brought to the classroom. The research of Baumrind (1991) indicates that the way parents raise their children influences personal development and usually determines children's attitudes toward school, teachers, grades, and motivation, which usually lasts through adulthood. A few examples of the roles that parents have played in helping their children to become successful are the following: Tiger Woods' father started teaching him how to play golf at age two; Donald Trump was taught the real estate business at a young age by his father; Donald Trump is continuing this trend with his daughter and his son; George W. Bush took up the presidential position that was held previously by his father; Serena and Venus Williams were taught the game of tennis at the tender ages of nine and ten by their father; Ben Carson, early on an unmotivated ghetto youth, describes in his book, "Gifted Hands," how his single, uneducated mother played the most important role in his becoming one of the most respected neurosurgeons in the world (Carson & Murphey,1990); President Obama often mentions how his single mother would get him up at four or five in the morning and make him read; Our 66th Secretary of State, Condoleezza Rice, has given credit to her parents for her success; Judge Sonia Sotomayor, Supreme Court nominee, made the following statement about her mother, "I have often said that I am all I am because of her, and I am only half the woman she is" (Shane & Fernandez, 2009). Her single mother raised her and her brother, who is a doctor, in a housing project in the Bronx. And, of course, there are thousands more, who, regardless of socioeconomic status, have been positively influenced by their parents and have become productive citizens.

During my 25 years as a school counselor, at times serving four schools simultaneously (a different school every day), I was in and out of thousands of classrooms and homes of students where I met with teachers, parents, and students. Following are my observations and experiences regarding these contacts.

Since every child has a constitutional right to a free education, it stands to reason that anyone who interferes with this right is abusing the child's constitutional right to his or her free education. Thus no person (including a parent) should be allowed to interfere in any way with the education of a child. I consider not giving that child what he or she needs to be successful in school is interfering with his/her education. With the above point of view in mind, some of the following solutions would entail passing legislation. Most of the parents do not see the value of our educational system. Nearly one third of the students who enter high school will not graduate in four years, and the dropout rate increases to about half for cultural minorities (Swanson, 2004). My theory is that in some cases, our system previously failed the parents, and they see that it has not improved for their children. I base my beliefs on the lack of interest and support that they show in their child's education. Below is a list of examples as to why I came to this conclusion and solutions for these concerns:

Concern
Parents do not attend parent meetings, conferences, and workshops.

For example, a school with an enrollment of 600 students may have less than 100 parents present at a parent meeting and/or workshop, yet our parenting center provides transportation for those parents who need it. In fact, several schools have parent advocates (people who are hired to specifically meet the needs of parents) who will transport parents to meetings; however, even with these available means of transportation, attendance by parents is extremely low. These results are based on my previous schools which were all Title I Schools.

*Note- The suggested mandatory workshops for uncooperative parents are one of the factors that school officials and politicians need to lobby into legislation. This requirement for parents should have been included in the No Child Left Behind Act. The No Child Left Behind Act (federal law) requires school systems meet annual benchmarks in areas including test scores and attendance (Morrison 2009).

Solution

Eliminate busing and replace it with neighborhood schools, to enable the parents to become involved with the school; thus transportation will not be a problem.

Concern
Parents will not give correct phone numbers to school officials.

Schools require at least four numbers where a parent can be reached in case of an emergency. Shortly after the start of school, my faculties and I discovered numbers that were given by parents were wrong or later exchanged for a private number. In some instances, the child does not know the number and/or was told not to give the number. This usually predicts the likelihood of the child experiencing academic difficulty and/ or behavior problems. In many circumstances, I had to suspend a child to make contact with the parent.

Solution

If incorrect contact information became a general practice of the parent, he/she would be fined, and the money would go to the school for tutorial services.

Parent would attend a mandatory workshop concerning how to coordinate home and school.

Concern
Parents will wait until the end of school year to complain about a child's failing grades.

There is no reason why a parent should not be aware of his or her child's progress. Open House is scheduled at the beginning of the school year, and parents are given the opportunity to meet their child's teacher(s) and to be informed about their child's curriculum for the school year. Also, meetings and/or conferences are hosted for the convenience of the parents. Moreover, academic deficiency notices are sent home three weeks prior to report cards being sent, and daily assignments including homework are to be signed for by parents. Finally, parents can communicate with teachers by letter, phone, face to face, and e-mail.

Solution

If a lack of communication becomes a general practice of the parent, he/she would be fined and the money would go to the school for tutorial services for his/her child.

Parent would attend a mandatory workshop concerning how to coordinate home and school.

Concern
Parents do not supply child with basic supplies (pencil and paper) and/or appropriate clothing (uniforms and coats).

Solution

If inappropriate clothing and lack of basic supplies becomes a general practice of the parent, he/she would be fined. The money would be used to pay for supplies and appropriate clothing for the student. This would also be reported to Juvenile Court and the Department of Child Protective Services whether or not the parent is receiving financial support from the federal government.

Parent would attend a mandatory workshop concerning how to coordinate home and school.

Concern
Parents will not register their child on the designated registration date. Some will bring students up to two weeks after the official start of school.

The start of a new school year is aired on all local news stations, announced by local newspapers, and posted on school billboards. Parents may call the school board or their child's school to receive a school calendar of the events for the upcoming school year.

Solution

Parent will be charged $10 per day for each day after the designated registration date. The money would go for tutorial services to bring student up to date on missed assignments. This would also be reported to Juvenile Court and the Department of Child Protective Services whether or not the parent is receiving financial support from the federal government.

Parent would attend a mandatory workshop concerning how to coordinate home and school.

Concern
Parents teach children to disrespect teachers by degrading teachers in the presence of their children.

Solution

Parents would attend a mandatory workshop concerning how to coordinate home and school.

Concern
Parents do not designate a place in the home for students to study or do homework.

Solution

Parents would attend a mandatory workshop regarding how to improve and coordinate home and school relationships. Based on the research of Garcia, the following benefits result from home-school cooperating: Improved attendance, better graduation rates, higher long-term achievement, greater enrollment in postsecondary education, positive attitudes and behavior (2004).

Concern
Parents allow poor attendance and excessive tardiness.

This results in poor work habits, freedom to become involved with crime, and lost and/or weakened academic skills. I recently read about a juvenile court judge who sentenced a mother of a second grader to 48 hours in jail for not getting her child to school. This parent was given an opportunity to defend herself and bring in doctors' notes. Her excuses were not supported by law. In the article, the school leaders stated, "They were forced to crack down on parents of truant students because federal law requires schools to have high attendance rates." The No Child Left Behind Act requires that schools and systems meet annual benchmarks in areas including test scores and attendance (Morrison, 2009).

Solution

The above- mentioned school leaders partnered with their local judges and drafted some polices to reflect the requirement of No Child Left Behind (Morrison, 2009).

The law states that parents who have children of compulsory school age are responsible for sending their children to school on a regular basis (Section 7, Education Act 1996).

The local authority may take legal action against parents if children do not attend regularly and the absences are not approved by the school system. The range of actions is as follows:

A penalty notice issued under the local Code of Conduct (Sections 444A and 444B, Education Act 1996): $50.00 fine paid within 28 days, rising to $100.00 within 29-42 days.

Parental Prosecution under Section 444(1) Education Act 1996: If a compulsory school age child who is registered as a student at a school fails to attend regularly, his/her parent may be found guilty of an offence for which the maximum fine is $1,000.00.

Prosecution under Section 444(1A), Education Act 1996 (as amended by Section109, Education and Inspections Act 2006): If a parent knows his/her child is failing to attend school on a regular basis and fails to cause him/her to do so, the parent is guilty of an offence, unless he/she can justify lack of attendance. Based on the above situation, a warrant can be issued to make a parent attend court, whereupon if a parent is found guilty, the maximum fine is $2,500.00 and/or a sentence up to 3 months in jail. Non-payment will result in a prosecution for the original offence.

Education Supervision Order (Section 447, Education Act 1996; Section 36, Children Act 1996): Makes the local authority responsible for advising, supporting, and giving directions to the supervised child and parent to make sure that the child is receiving a suitable education. Parent will become guilty of an offence if he/she persistently fails to comply with reasonable directions, and the maximum fine is $1,000.00.

Enforce the law.

Concern
Parents will transfer students several times during the school year.

One of my most extreme cases involved a first grader who had attended seven different schools while still in the first grade. The average number of transfers during elementary school is three to four. A high rate of mobility is a contributing factor to the dropout rate of students from unstable families (Barton, 2006).

Solution

Parents would only be allowed to transfer a student at the end of a semester and must give a satisfactory reason why a student can not continue in the present school.

Concern

Parents will ignore teachers' requests for conferences, academic deficiency notices, phone calls, letters and any other forms of communication regarding their child.

My only means of getting the attention of some parents was through suspension of the child.

Solution

If parents display unwillingness to work with the teacher to help improve their children's poor academic status and/or behavioral problems, they will be fined. The money will go to the child's school for tutorial services. Once students begin to receive satisfactory grades, the fine will cease. Family psychologist, John Rosemond, author of "Living with Children," expressed in his column, "Teachers need backup from parents if the system is to work" (2008). He stated many teachers have told him that not only do so many parents not support them, but a good number will respond by accusing those teachers of creating the problem in the first place. In other words, the teacher is chastised if the child misbehaves. However, students make good progress, regardless of their race, ethnicity, or the education or income of their parents if parents are fully involved with their children's education. Other benefits of parental involvement are students' grades and tests are higher, homework is consistently done, attendance is regular, behavior is positive, and parents gain respect from their children's teachers (U.S. Department of Education, 2001).

Parent would attend a mandatory workshop concerning how to coordinate home and school.

Concern
Kindergarten students are enrolled academically and socially unprepared for school.

Kindergarten is the foundation of all the other grades, yet parents bring students and place them in kindergarten without previous school-related experiences. According to Piaget, experience is the key to the cognitive development of a child (1970). Development does not occur in human beings without experience. This presents the teacher with the problem of playing "catch up". This is virtually impossible taking into consideration the following three factors: the teacher has an inflexible timeframe to meet goals (180 days), the parent is unwilling to become academically involved, and there is a lack of moral support from home. I realize that every parent can not help his or her child academically. However, teachers can work with a child who is sent to school ready to learn. This means that the parent is willing to work with the teacher and provide his or her child with moral support.

Let's briefly examine why Asian American kindergarteners and first grade students on average show higher reading and mathematic achievement than other cultures (Denton & West, 2002). According to Choa (2000), Asian American parents, based on their tradition, have respect for authority and value education. Goyette & Xie (1999) found that Asian American parents highly value education as a means to a successful lifestyle. Based on these two factors, they use a direct-hands on approach regarding their children's education. They teach and/or tutor their children as well as participate in school activities (Choa, 2000). The activities that are not directly related to academics such as watching television, video games or playing with friends are limited (Choi, Bempechat & Ginsburg, 1994). Asian American parents engage their children in school-related activities such as learning to play an instrument, art, reading, language and math. These parents feel that it is the teacher's responsibility to run the classroom and it is their responsibility to assist the teacher in academically preparing their children at home.

Solution

Require Mandatory Pre-Kindergarten Summer School for any child (lacking academic readiness skills) entering kindergarten and include parenting workshops. The two main goals of this school are: To make sure that these students are ready for kindergarten/school (to prevent "catch up") and to inform and engage parents in the forthcoming curriculum. Some years ago, we had an early childhood program that allowed for homemakers to visit the homes of parents to educate parents in strategies to provide academic readiness for school. A similar program was hasted in North Carolina based on the following components: parenting lesson, a language-oriented preschool program, nutritional and social services from birth (Jacobsen, 2003). The children who attended scored higher on achievement and intelligence assessments compared to non-participants. I believe we need to return to this practice with the Mandatory Pre-Kindergarten Summer School because young children benefit from learning-related experiences (McDevitt & Ormond, 2007).

How do school board members factor into the equation of the problems?

Many, board members are not qualified to serve; moreover, many are unaware of the needs of our children, parents, and teachers. How did I come to this conclusion? By way of all the illogical decisions that have negatively affected our children's education. (Examples of poor administrative decisions are listed on the following pages).

The majority of the students' reading and math skills do not reflect their actual grade level. Teachers' morale is low due to the excessive amount of paperwork (filling out reports, doing surveys and many other administrative duties) and unruly students. Indeed, after teaching for five years, 46% of new teachers leave the teaching profession (Kober, 2006).

In the world of sports and big business, leaders and board members are carefully selected. A coach is not going to be permitted to stay if he or she fails repeatedly to make the play-off. Board members who serve million/billion dollar companies are going to be well-informed, knowledgeable and worthy of serving on that board. If they cause the company to lose money or stunt the growth of that company, they are quickly removed. In my opinion, it is unreasonable to allow anyone to serve our children without possessing exemplary leadership skills and a body of knowledge that can be used to make positive decisions for our children and teachers under normal conditions and during critical times.

Teachers are college graduates, must pass several tests, are required to regularly attend professional development workshops/meetings, are continuously monitored and evaluated, and are given three years to prove themselves only to have someone who does not have a fraction of their knowledge make decisions regarding their work. This could be compared to placing people on medical boards without any knowledge of medicine.

Standards of excellence in the educational field are no different than for the world of business. If the board of directors of a corporation declines to guarantee that a sound governing model is in place and operating conscientiously and effectively, it is only inviting the collapse of the enterprise it oversees.

I have listed a few of the devastating mistakes that have been made due to the absence of a knowledge base in one large school district. Our children continue to pay dearly for these mistakes.

1. The mission statement that was adopted, "Every Day Every Child College Bound" completely ignored the thousands of students who are not going to attend college. This statement did not show any concern for or interest in those students who graduated with a Special Education Diploma and/or a Certificate of Attendance (those students who did not pass the Gateway -exit test) or those students whose career choices do not require a college education. According to statistics regarding my district, only 69% of the students graduated with a diploma (TDOE Report Card, 2007), and of course all diplomas do not lead to college. This mission statement should have read, "Meeting the Needs of Every Child Every Day".

As a middle school counselor helping students with their 4 Plus Career Plan, I had many students share with me that they felt "left out." They stated that the only students who got attention were the "smart ones." This may be one of the reasons why 25,823 students were suspended and/or expelled from the system (TDOE Report Card, 2007). Indeed, my students along with many others did not show any interest in their 4 Plus Career Plan. The 4 Plus Career Plan is important because it prepares students for the world in which they will be a participating citizen. The document is to assist students and their parents with planning their high school course-work and their future endeavors. The students and their parents are to select the course of study (minimum, college, or vocational) that will best prepare the students for their career choice. The selection of the course work is extremely important because of the consequences on future career choices. For example, a student who desires to be a doctor or an attorney needs to enroll in courses that will lead to college. Unfortunately, if this does not happen, the student will have a very difficult task making a satisfactory score on the aptitude exams. This in turn, makes it almost impossible to be accepted by a college. If a student is accepted, he/she will have an arduous road ahead because the chosen high school course-work did not provide him/her with the necessary foundation to lead to a successful outcome.

The involvement of my students' parents in the 4 Plus Career Plan was little to none, which explains why our students' interest level was low. A parent's attitudes and values shape the way students think about school and academic accomplishment (Tompkins, 2006). Furthermore, parents' expectations and attitudes regarding education are transferred through their involvement with educational activities and/or tasks such as the 4 Plus Career Plan. All parents were required to sign this document, but the only means that we had to guarantee signatures was to ban participation in the eighth grade graduation ceremony. This worked for signatures only, but still we did not get a high level of interest from parents or students. Ironically, the eighth grade graduation ceremony is a well-attended, high dollar occasion. Parents spend money on elaborate dresses and suits in spite of the fact that their children have exhibited low academic performance for the last nine years of school.

Solution

My solution to this problem is my "Meeting the Needs of Every Child Every Day Curriculum". A general overview of this curriculum is listed under that heading, toward the end of this section.

2. Our system adopted a reading program that was designed to allow each school to select its own individual reading program. Each reading program was unique to an individual school regarding goals, objectives and grading system. However, when there was a lack of coordination among the programs, and every school was knowledgeable only about their own reading program it did not account for a highly mobile student population. For example, a fourth grader at Red School was reading on a second grade level and making good grades on this level. When that student moved to Blue school, the teacher assumed that he was a good reader on a fourth grade level since his true reading grade level was not indicated on his report card. The student's subsequent poor performance caused the teacher to become confused, and she referred him to me (counselor) for academic screening. This

trend occurred all over the system as student after student was referred. For example, a first grader who transferred to my school was referred to me for screening as he was experiencing academic difficulty; however he had attended seven different schools during his time in first grade. No-one took into consideration the high mobility rate of our students. When they leave a school after six weeks or less and attend another school with a different reading program, this caused the students and the teachers at their new schools serious problems. This was a disaster.

Solution

There should be a district-wide reading and math curriculum that has the same goals, objectives, and grading system at each school to provide all students with coherence and stability. This would enable teachers to begin where the student had ended in his or her previous school.

3. The Blue Ribbon Plan was designed to take the place of corporal punishment; however, there was no trial and error period. Corporal punishment ended in June 2005, and the Blue Ribbon Plan began in August 2005 and was implemented system-wide in less than two months. In June, 2005 all faculty members from all schools were required to attend a two day summit, whose purpose was for each school to develop a plan that excluded corporal punishment and yet reduced the number of office referrals and suspensions. The Blue Ribbon Plan was deadly for the teachers. This bogged teachers down with unnecessary amounts of paperwork and took away valuable instructional time. Each intervention that a teacher tried had to be documented before he/she could refer a child to the counselor and office. Students became aware that there were no real consequences for their unruly behavior and took advantage of it. The Blue Ribbon Plan gave the teachers the blues (Aarons, 2007a).

Solution

The following solution can and should be used for all new programs. Two groups-- control and experimental-- should be selected on a pilot basis in at least two different schools before implementing any program into the entire system. Lots of valuable time and money have been wasted without prior sampling of programs.

Next, a trial and error period at selected schools should have identified and eliminated the kinks; then the program could have been implemented system wide. Or another solution could have been to survey all parents regarding corporal punishment. For example, during registration, have parents check whether or not they want their child to receive corporal punishment for this school year. Those who did not want their child to receive corporal punishment would be requested to state what type of discipline works best for their child. This would help the school to meet the needs of each individual child.

4. Selection of Superintendents- Our two former superintendents came from districts that did not have similar problems or similar student population. And in keeping with the trend, the last choice is also from out of town and out of touch. Our district is large with a majority of African American students of low socioeconomic status. I feel that the superintendents did not understand the needs of our children or our city. If they had, the previously mentioned programs and plans would not have been selected. Specifically, they implemented programs that had not been well-thought out and that were mismatches for our children. These factors detrimentally affected our children's education, their future endeavors, and our city. Indeed, these programs literally brought the system to its knees. When this occurred, both superintendents left without being considerate enough to wait for their positions to be filled.

Solution

Closely review and give great consideration to candidates who have a history in our system. Our superintendent should be extremely knowledgeable of the different cultures of our children, the value system of our parents, and the needs of our students as well as our city. Some candidates, who were not considered, in my opinion, would have been a great asset to our system as they came up through the ranks. I know of one candidate in particular who started her career as a teacher assistant. She is now serving as one of our most distinguished principals in a school that experiences the types of problems that occur system-wide. Her experiences empower her to know the authentic needs of our students.

Is money the answer to our problems? Are our board members managing our tax dollars in ways that are the most beneficial to our children and teachers?

No, is the answer to both questions. Pouring money into a system that continuously mismanages it will never solve the problem. Our politicians deeply believe that money is the answer to our educational problems yet, the budget of some school systems is almost twice the budget for the city (Vergos, 2007). However, in my opinion, lack of money is the least of our problems. Quite simply, the money that is available for the students usually does not make it to the correct destination. So much of taxpayers' hard earned money is wasted. Why? The socioeconomic status of most, if not all, previous and present board members is either blue collar or middle class. How can we expect them to read with understanding and manage millions of dollars for an agency with which that they have little or no previous experience?

I have taken the liberty to list several examples of mismanagement and pure waste:

- Busing, which was established to assist with the integration of the school system, continues without a cause. The schools have mostly African American students . Could the reason for the busing be for the sake of diversity? Not when we are busing African American students to be with African American students who are of the same economical status and culture.

Solution

Neighborhood schools will save million of dollars and allow parents and the community to become directly involved with their children's school. The parents' excuse of not having transportation for not attending school functions would no longer exist. Also, bus riders miss before and after school programs that could provide the necessary tutoring to help them raise a grade or pass a subject. Additionally, according to research, students who participate in extracurricular activities tend to be more motivated and get higher grades than those who don't (Black, 2002). Unfortunately, bus riders miss the opportunity to engage in such beneficial activities.

- The board spent approximately $30 million on a plan to reshape the attendance boundaries of almost 100 schools without doing their homework and refused to listen to input from citizens who lived in the neighborhoods that were going to be directly affected. These citizens informed the board that the change would end in tragedy based on the continued rivalry of the gangs who are actively present in their neighborhoods. And, naturally, the most possible situation occurred where a student lost his life and others went to jail (Roberts, 2009a).

- There was an incidence of $17 million no–bid school contracts with a bus company (Perrusquia & Goetz, 2007).

- DirecTV is enjoyed by those who have offices and use conference rooms (The Commercial Appeal, 2007).

- Approximately $90,000 was spend on professional development and travel for chosen employees. One top-ranking administrator attended seven seminars. (The Commercial Appeal, 2007).

- An alternative middle school program cost more than 4 million dollars over a four year period, which board members had thought would be virtually free (Kumar, 2005).

- No explanation was given as to why a high school auditorium construction went from $1 million to $5 million (Vergos, 2007).

- The school system's nutrition center personnel hosted a party that cost $600 for food and $2,400.00 in labor and resulted in a spoiled food incident that cost the school system more than $3.7 million (Goetz, 2007; Aarons, 2007b).

- Some furniture cost $86,000 to replace furniture that was already in place (The Commercial Appeal, 2007).

- Non-necessary positions were created with salaries averaging more than $100,000 (Memphis City Schools System, 2007).

- Several millions have been spent for consulting contracts (most from out of state) that have basically led nowhere (Vergos, 2007). After all this very expensive consulting, we still require comprehensive strategies for addressing the needs of approximately 25, 000 students who are over age for their grade level (Roberts, 2008 b).

- And last but not least, a bill accrued of over $600,000 for cell phones that were used for matters other than the educational needs of our students (Roberts, 2009b).

These few incidents cause one to wonder where the board of education members were when these incidents occurred. My main concern is our board members did not come to our children's rescue. Why did they sit idly by and allow these incidents to occur? Our school system continues to poorly-prepare our students for bright futures. Apparently, these plans and programs were accepted without any questions being asked. Most of our members have served on the board for years and should have been aware of the pejorative effect that these programs/plans would have on our children's education and thus their future.

Ruling out any possible incompetencey is basic to ensuring that every child's welfare and education come first. I firmly believe that the board members have an important responsibility to assist in the education of our students, and the responsibility for the system rests on them. This means that the members cannot be passive observers any more than parents can afford to allow their small children to be unsupervised while playing outside. Both amount to negligence and can lead to danger. Members of the board should have spoken up against the mission statement, should have objected to the reading programs. It is an unfortunate fact that some members are negligent in this way, but most of their neglect is unintentional. They are unaware of what it takes to operate a school and most important the formula for educating a student to be successful in society. Most members literally walk in off the streets into the position. They do not know the reality of school life. They sit on the board for months, even years without assuming real ownership or educating themselves to the facts of school life. They never understand that the system's life is in their hands, that responsibility for its survival and its success lies with them. Before a member can consistently act in the best interest of our school system, each member must understand and accept responsibility for the system's success or failure.

Solution

Those who are sincerely interested in the future of our children should work toward a clear understanding of our children's needs for them to become valuable and successful citizens in the United States. As it stands, in some districts, just about anyone can be a member of the board as long as they have a desire to be one. And to add to this, voter turnout for the elections is extremely low. I strongly feel that along with that desire, members should have a knowledge base upon which to draw when there are ill-defined problems and major decisions to be made, especially those that will directly impact our students' future achievement and status of living.

Below are the steps that I feel are necessary to be an Effective Board Member.

1. ***School Experience***- Spend a total of eight (8) weeks observing and actively participating in each grade level of the school. This will include pre-school, elementary, middle, high and all special programs. Make sure that you are there for the beginning, middle and the end of a school year. Become knowledgeable about how a school operates during the entire school day and witness first-hand the trials and tribulations of life in a classroom and a school. Circulate among the entire faculty and all associated workers (librarian, counselor, facilitator, principal, assistant principal, psychologist, social worker, parents, bus driver, etc.) to fully understand their missions, and observe. You should be equipped with pen and paper and feel free to ask questions.

2. ***Course Work***- I highly recommend enrolling in the following four courses: Human development, diversity, school curriculum, and finance. Human development and diversity courses will help you to understand how students develop and how everyone is different. This will allow you to become knowledgeable about the different cultures and what value the families place on education. This is critical in order to meet student individual needs. The school curriculum course will help you to understand the tremendous

and most demanding job that teachers must perform to teach based on students' development, needs, and the demands of the curriculum (goals, objectives and standards) within the stipulated 180 day period. Based on the fact that the average person is not accustomed to managing million of dollars, the finance course will help build knowledge of how to read, understand, and manage large sums of money. There should be a transparent online system where taxpayers at the stroke of a key seven days a week would be informed of how their tax dollars are being spent. Also, they should be able to voice their opinion regarding the rationale behind the spending.

3. *Assessment*- An exam would be given based on the four courses of study mentioned above.

4. *Certificate*-Upon the accumulation of the required school experience hours, completion of the course work and successfully passing the exam, a certificate would be awarded. This would be a requirement before running for a position on the board of education. If you feel these steps are asking too much, ask yourself whether you would want someone making a decision about your health who has a very limited amount of knowledge about health. Or would you want someone without a law degree representing your legal case in the courtroom? Likewise, how knowledgeable do you want your pilot to be?

Is the size of the district part of the problem?

Yes!

Here are six factors that I feel have a bearing on the operation of the district:

1. The district has serious problems.
2. No one person can be an expert in everything or be in all places.
3. We have a large student body and many employees other than teachers.
4. It is bureaucratic and hierarchical. These produce two negative factors: Teachers feel nameless and faceless, and they are not considered to be part of the decision-making process.
5. Getting things accomplished takes time.

Solution

Down size the district. Based on these six factors, the district needs to be divided into three to function to its full potential: It is overwhelming and nearly impossible to expect one person to be able to handle everything. He or she cannot possibly pay attention to all details. The district should be divided into pre-school/elementary, middle, and high school districts, each with its own superintendent and board of education. Each superintendent and board would be very knowledgeable of their children's growth, development, and needs. Along with this knowledge, each superintendent should possess classroom experience with the age groups of students in his/ her jurisdiction. This would help to assure that the superintendent would have a clear understanding of what the teachers are faced with daily and the needs of their students. Moreover, teachers work much better under the leadership of an instructional leader who "has been there and done that" (Harris & Lowery, 2002). Therefore, that person should have an in-depth understanding of the needs of the students, parents, teachers, and principals. Teachers want someone who takes a hands-on approach to the teaching-learning process. The hands-on approach would allow each superintendent to become directly involved with his or her schools. The superintendent can be an eyewitness to the good, bad, and ugly events that occur during a regular school day. The hands-on approach would also allow the superintendent to participate in the celebratory and problem-solving phases of ongoing events. Meanwhile, teachers, parents, students, and principals would serve as executive staff to their superintendent without pay; the payoff would be in meeting the needs of the staff (faculty) in a positive and timely manner. This down-sizing would make for a more manageable system and allow for more accountability and transparency. This also provides for built-in checks and balances. For example, all would know immediately who will be held accountable for a group of elementary students who are entering middle school with weak reading skills.

Will this cost the taxpayer more money?

I don't believe it will. The following is an example of an overloaded superintendent's staff: deputy superintendent, two associate superintendents, three executive directors, one director and two chiefs. Superintendents in large districts (such as ours) results in salaries that are considerably higher than small districts. They can make from $200,000 up to $500,000 plus benefits and perks (Swanson, 2006).

Also, many other positions could be eliminated and/or combined. The two groups of the hardest working people in the schools are the teachers and the principals. Since teachers are considered in loco parentis; they have total responsibility (academic, social, emotional, physical, and psychological) for their 25-30 students for six hours five days a week. In addition, the principals are held responsible for every person who works in their school, every child who attends their school, and every parent who has a child in their school. My question is what could keep a person (superintendent) busy eight hours five days a week if they do not have the prosed responsibilities?

The deputy's, the two associate superintendents', the three executive directors' the director's, and the two chiefs' time could be much better spent using hands-on approach in the schools.

Are school uniforms really uniforms?

A student came into my office because, according to her, a strange man had followed her to school and he was trying to convince her to get into his car. This was a sixth grade female student whose school uniform skirt was so short and tight that she could not bend over without showing her underwear. I called the mother and informed her of the incident, indicating that this incident was not her daughter's fault. However, I explained the child's attire may have sent the wrong message to this person. If you look around the schools, you will quickly notice that the only thing our students' uniforms have in common is the shade of color. In some cases, uniforms are too baggy, too tight, too short, or have extra details. Male students were often sent to me for belts because they could not walk two steps without their pants falling off their posterior. There is nothing uniform about students' uniforms currently, and overall, they do not suggest professionalism.

Webster's New World Dictionary defines a uniform as "always the same, not varying, having the same form, appearance, and manner. The official or distinctive clothes or outfit worn conforming to a given standard by the member of a particular group, as police officers or soldiers".

While vacating in the Bahamas, I noticed that students were in uniforms all exactly alike in color (including shade) and detail. In contrast, our students' uniforms have no standards. The colors vary in shades as well as details, and the clothing does not display unity or sense of readiness for an academic day.

Solution

The system should contract out to one company for school uniforms just as they contract out for buses, which themselves have a uniform look; no-one has a problem recognizing a school bus. Such a policy would set a standard, and our students would appear ready to learn and professional. I would also suggest seamstresses be available to alter uniforms and ensure appropriate fit.

Should every student attend college?

"Every Day Every Child College Bound"

The mission statement, "Every Day Every Child College Bound," that has been used by the city schools for the last several years has always disturbed me and other educators. Those of us who work daily with students know that a great number of them will not attend college. Misguidedly, our system as well as others worked toward every student going to college. Indeed, the curriculum and everyone's attention are based on students attending college. However, over 70,000 students are at least two years below grade level in reading and math, only 69% of the student population in the city graduated, and 93% from the county graduated (TDOE Report Card, 2007). Finally, only 66.9% of the 2004 class graduated in 2008(Roberts, 2008a). This includes special education students and students who have received the Certificate of Attendance (I attended school but I do not have any skills) with diplomas and certificates that do not entitle them to college as an option. Also, the school systems are too diverse to promote college for every child. Furthermore, the dropout rate is overwhelming for our African American males. Barber & McClellan (1987), surveyed 17 major metropolitan districts to have the districts list reasons students gave for dropping out of school. Among the top reasons were lack of interest and boredom with school. The research of Gewertz suggests that motivation is a major reason in dropping out. In his study, 69% of dropouts stated they were not invigorated or motivated to work diligently, two thirds indicated they were not challenged and almost half said their classes lack interest (2006).

Nationwide, 69% of African American children in America cannot read at grade level 4, and only 45% of African American men graduate from high school in the United States (Clay & Johnson, 2008). My questions are the following: So what does the mission statement insinuate to the students who are not interested in college careers or who do not qualify for college? Is there anything in place for those students who want careers that do not require college? Their only clear alternative is technical school; however, the enrollment in technical schools is extremely low (TDOE Report Card, 2008). If you are a non-college student because you have been tracked into a non-college curriculum, or your career of choice does not require a college degree, where do you go from here, to a minimum wage job or a career of crime? Are we leaving such students without incentive to work toward a diploma? My former students believed that their school system had ignored them. In turn, they are being rejected by society because they do not have any skills and/or an education that will allow them to be successful in the workplace. Clearly, our system has failed them. As a result of this, our city is paying a high cost by not being able to attract the big businesses to grow financially. We do not attract successful people who have a desire to invest in our city. Businesses such as Dell Computers (selected Nashville, Tennessee) and Toyota Motor Corporation (selected Mississippi) have often opted for other cities and states because they have stated that we do not have a pool of skilled workers, college graduates or qualified employees. Raymond Walker, an Atlanta-based site selection consultant stated "Memphis fell off the "50 Hottest Cites" list. We've heard recently that the quality of the workforce isn't as good as it is in some other locations"(Watson, 2003). In announcing Tupelo as the winning site, Toyota officials repeatedly emphasized the area's quality workforce, saying the labor pool was "educated, ethical and friendly with a strong work ethic- a perfect match for the "Toyota way" (Maki, 2007).

A trend of selecting out-of-town people was supported three consecutive times by our board of education's decision to select the last three superintendents from other states and to hire out-of-state consulting agencies (Vergos, 2007). Several qualified candidates who have worked their way up through the ranks of our school system and who were very familiar with the needs of our children and city were not selected. Our citizens can bear witness to the deleterious consequences of the last two superintendents. These consequences included the following: high drop out rate, increases in the number of Title I Schools, three quarters of the students being two or more grade levels below their grade levels in reading and math, the millions of dollars wasted instead of being used to help meet the needs of our children and teachers, the impossible demands placed on our teachers that led to low morale, the increase in school violence, the decrease in safety for students and teachers, programs mismatched for our students, unqualified personnel placed in high ranking positions, top heavy unjustifiable administration whose qualifications and salary are not justified, nepotism being valued above the needs of our children and teachers, cover-up of criminal and sexual misconduct, retaliation of those who stood up for their rights, and failure to focus on one of our most major concerns: students' parents. And of course, once the consequences have permeated our entire system, they leave the students in a pool of ignorance. For without the knowledge that students so badly need, there is only a dim future. Judge Greg Mathis points out that, "There are over a million African American men incarcerated in the nation, and approximately 700,000 prisoners are released from prison every year. The majority of them are uneducated or undereducated and have limited job skills" (Waldron, 2008). Our students are included in these statistics. According to information gathered by Juvenile Intervention & Faith (JIFF), "Young people, especially African American children are flooding the halls, lobbies, and detention centers of juvenile court at the rate of 23,000 cases in 2005" (Carr, 2009). Another option, the military, is also off limits to many African American children. The Department of Education revealed a report concluding 75% of our America youth (ages 17-24) are unable to enlist in the United States military because they fail to graduate high school, have a criminal record, or are physically unfit. U.S. Secretary of Education, Arne Duncan, former NATO Supreme Commander, Gerral Wesley Clark, and some of American's top retired admirals, generals, and other military leaders called for immediate action to address this threat to America's national security (US Newswire, 2009).

Another example of our city's lack of qualified employees is shown by our police department efforts to recruit our young people to be police officers. The department's pool of qualified recruits was at a bare minimum and many complaints were made by local citizens about the lack of hiring of African American youth. The department's answer to the complaint was the candidates failed to meet the two basic requirements: 1.You can not have any felony convictions. 2. You must pass the entrance exam (These are the same requirements for college).

Dan Randall, manager of Priority Solutions, a third-party logistics provider in Memphis, made the following statements, "Because we distribute pharmaceutical samples, we require extensive background and drug checks." He said, "We see applicants who are 17, 18, and 19 with felonies on their records. We can't hire them" (Roberts, 2006).

We are presently experiencing an educational and economic crisis, which calls for effective reform. Based on my observations, my research, the research of others, and expert opinions, I firmly believe that the curriculum should be changed to accommodate the needs of all of our students. For years educators have been aware of the diversity among our students. This diversity includes culture, abilities, learning styles, and interest. The crisis that we are experiencing demands that our educators, political leaders, and citizens examine non-traditional "out of the box" programs and curriculums to help us meet the needs of our diverse student body.

The six determinants that have influenced my beliefs follow:

1. In 1983, a Harvard University Professor, Dr. Howard Gardner, defined intelligence as the ability to solve problems or to create products that are valued within one or more cultural settings (Gardner 1983, 2000). Based on his definition of intelligence, he developed the theory of 8 different types of intelligence. They are linguistic (good with words), logical-mathematics (good with reasoning/numbers), spatial (good with pictures) bodily kinesthetic (good control over your body), musical (good with music), interpersonal (good people skills), intrapersonal (self-awareness) and naturalist (good knowledge of nature). In other words, we are all intelligent in different ways. Dr. Gardner pointed out that emphasis is placed on people who are intelligent in linguistic and logical-mathematical abilities, based on a very narrow definition of what intelligence is. However, he feels that all types of intelligence should receive equal attention (1993). Deplorably, most of our students who possess the other six types intelligence do not have their needs addressed. And they usually qualify for some degree of special education services. I have witnessed students who struggled with language and numbers yet who were excellent musicians and artists. There are millionaires/billionaires, successful business-people, who were judged to be failures at school. For example, Bill Gates, Microsoft founder, owns billions of dollars, but he does not own a college degree. Many employment experts believe that a college degree is not needed to be successful. According to data from the U.S. Department of Labor, 2008, there are hundreds of jobs with high paying salaries that do not require a four year college degree. And of course, if everyone goes to college, who would fill the non-college positions? Moncarz and Crosby, economists in the Office of Occupational Statistics and Employment Projection, BLS has stated, "Between 2002 and 2010, job openings for workers who are entering an occupation for the first time and who don't have a bachelor's degree are expected to total roughly 42

million. About 27 million of these openings are expected to be held by workers who have high school diploma or less education (2005).

My proposed curriculum would empower teachers to present topics using a variety of teaching strategies. The antiquated ways of presenting information through dull lectures that cause our students to become so bored that they drop out of school would be obsolete. The new approach would include but not be limited to role playing, music, cooperative learning, shadowing, field trips, and authentic tasks. This non- traditional "out of the box curriculum" could give our school system the face lift it needs to solve the educational crisis that is foreshadowing a dim future for our children and our nation. If the theory of multiple types of intelligence in combination with career awareness and development programs were employed, we could have an effective reform that would meet the needs of all of our students. This would lead each and every student to a productive life and strengthen our national economy.

2. My research was based on the fact that most urban elementary and early secondary school students are occupationally illiterate. Few know the meaning of work and jobs, the integral relationship of employment to the economics of our world society, the impact that the choice of work has on our lives, on the rewards of work as well as the preparation needed to cope with the frustration of work. This research shows that elementary (fourth grade) students after being involved in an authentic task related to a career were able to better understand the relationship of how the academic world relates to the world of work (Taylor, 1993). The evaluation studies and research done by Kazis & Goldberger (1995): and Stern (1995), indicate possible correlation between positive student outcomes and the structure that the employer and schools put into the work experiences. Unfortunately, our present school curriculum has failed to offer our students the needed exposure to the world of work and its relationship to education. Therefore, our students see no reason to excel in school. Work experience should become a general educational methodology rather than a special kind of educational program (Hoyt, 1981).

3. Lynch & Harnish (1998) found work-based learning as an educational approach uses the workplace to structure learning experiences that contribute to the intellectual, social, academic, and career development of students and supplements these with school activities that apply, reinforce, refine, or extend the learning that occurs at a workplace. By

so doing, students develop attitudes, knowledge, skills, insights, habits, and associations from both work and school experiences and are able to connect learning with real-life work activities.

4. Bailey's & Merritt's (1997) studies of work-based learning strategies yielded positive impact on student motivation, achievement, and continuation of education.

5. The Lowell Public Schools System in Lowell, Massachusetts established the City Magnet School (kindergarten through eight grades), which has a diverse student body and provides students with a strong traditional program in the basic skills (reading, writing, and math). In this magnet school, however, the students learn basic skills as they legislate, adopt budgets, pass tax measures, administer justice, govern, or simply communicate with one another regarding commercial and legal matters. They read, write, and use mathematics with purpose. The students at the City Magnet School generally test at the top of the Lowell school population on a variety of measures. Lowell's microsociety school educates children for the world they enter as adults (Lowell, 1989).

6. Michael Farr, LaVerne Ludden, and Laurence Shatkin are authors of "The 300 Best Jobs That Don't Require a Four Year Degree, (Farr, Ludden & Shatkin, 2003), and Michael Farr wrote "Top 100 Careers Without a Four-Year Degree" (Farr, 2009). Based on their latest findings, many great jobs pay well, offer growth, and do not require a four year college degree. For example, Harlow Unger's book, "But What If I Don't Want to Go to College? A Guide to Success Through Alternative Education" (Unger, 2006), states "that 56 million jobs will open up between now and 2012 of which 33.6 million will be replacements for retiring workers, and 22 million will be new jobs. Three quarters of those job openings do not require a four year college degree, only alternative career education or on-the-job training." He also stated that "there are over 50 million jobs that do not require a degree and pay upwards of $40,000 a year." The most important factor to employers is skills not degrees. This is due to our country being service-orientated and high tech. The Economic Policy Foundation, a non-profit agency based in Washington, D.C. found that in the near future, only 23% of the jobs available will require a college degree (Riley, 2008).

Unfortunately, our schools do not teach with the shifting workplace dynamic in mind. Instead, our schools place a great deal of attention on tracking. The original goal of tracking was to provide students with career choices other than college. However, it provides them very few choices and segregates the students narrowly into two groups (Oakes, 2005): those groups with bright futures (college bound) and those without bright futures (non-college bound). The non-college bound students are usually subject to limited vocational instruction and a curriculum that has much less to offer than the curriculum for the college bound students.

In summary, we need to open our minds to a more realistic way of educating all of our students. Thus, we need targeted methods to develop other types of intelligence and to make marketable the range of abilities that our students possess. Our students need to be honored for being the unique and special human beings that they are and nurtured for the greatest that they are capable of sharing with their fellow Americans. We, as United States citizens, are responsible for helping each and every child develop to full potential. This will lead to each child becoming a productive citizen, empowered to help maintain the dignity and strength of our nation. Keep in mind, the people who are the backbone of America, the people who keep our country going on a day to day basis often do not have jobs that require a four year college degree. However, what they do have are skills.

Below is an introduction to my proposed program:
Meeting the Needs of Every Child Every Day Program

Introduction

I assessed hundreds of students during my time as a counselor, and the majority of the students were reading and performing math at least two grade levels below their grade. Our school system has reported 25,000 students who are two or more grade levels below their grade in reading and/ or math and 9,000 are in elementary grades (Roberts, 2008a). Personally, I believe that the numbers go even higher. In fact, the majority of students who attend Title I Schools are usually two or more grade levels below their grade (U.S. Department of Education, 2009). At the present time we have 97 elementary schools out of 112 elementary schools that are Title I, 28 middle schools out of 36 that are Title I, and 30 high schools out of 35 that are Title I (Memphis City Schools, 2009). The other baggage that the students have is their parents showed little or no interest in their child's education.

Program

My program, Meeting the Needs of Every Child Every Day (MTNOECED) will insure that each child's individual needs are met before graduation. Upon graduation, each student will have a diploma and skills that will allow him or her to continue education in college or be ready to enter the world of work.

My program will allow these students to receive a diploma that will lead them to a better life filled with hope upon graduation. At graduation, honor students are applauded for receiving scholarships to different colleges, but no attention is given to the students who will not attend college. My program will honor and recognize those students who are receiving scholarships and those who will be walking into a good paying career. My program does not require any extra money and I propose it should begin with students in grade six (6) and continue through grade twelve (12). The communities, especially the business community, will be closely involved. Parents, students, and the communities will buy into this program due to the outstanding benefits each of these stakeholders will receive. It will motivate students to attend school, which in turn will eliminate many behavior problems in the system. According to Tennessee Department of Education Report Card (2007), 28,315 students in the city and county were suspended and expelled. The following lists the total number of suspensions and expulsions according to race: African American- 25,823, Hispanic- 480, and whites- 690. The drop out rate for city and county is 19.1 %. These students feel that they have nothing to lose and nothing to gain after attending schools for twelve years. During my 30 years with the school system as a professional school counselor, the majority of my clients were African American male students. These students were two or more years behind in reading and/or math, so they often met the requirements for special education placement. There was no college in their future or anything else worthwhile. Why? Our school systems did not provide them with a choice other than technical schools.

Below is a brief overview of the program:
1. All sixth graders who consistently scored low on standardized tests in reading and/or math and who consistently received low reading and/

or math grades would be placed in reading and math programs that are specific to their individual needs. The students would have their strengths and weaknesses addressed in each subject. Dan Randall, manager of Priority Solutions, a third-party logistics provider in Memphis, wants to put more focus on students in the middle grades, so they don't make the wrong decisions (Roberts, 2006).

2. They would be given an in-depth career inventory that would identify and match their strengths with their career interest (aptitude assessment). Many Japanese and European schools automatically test all 14 year olds to determine their aptitudes. These tests help determine those students who will be successful in college and those who need alternative form of education (career education) that refines those talents and ensures they will be successful and respected in their field (Unger, 2006).

3. These students would attend reading classes in the morning and math and technology classes in the afternoon four days a week. The goal of the reading, math, and technology curricula is to relate these basic academic subjects to the world of work. This goal would be accomplished through authentic (real world) tasks that the students would be able to relate to and understand.

4. On Fridays, students would attend a Career Awareness/ Development Class, and monthly they would be introduced to a variety of careers by way of resource people who would give presentations regarding their careers. The Career Awareness class would make the connection between school and the world of work. Meanwhile, students would be taken through all phases of the world of work as it relates to school, including work ethics. Indeed, students would be given hands-on experiences to physically and mentally involve them in every aspect of the world of work. This curriculum will be designed to teach them about the work force from beginning to end. Students would begin by reading the want ads; then, they would move through the interview process, being hired/fired, getting a promotion, retirement, and everything in between. A clear connection would be made among education, career, and living expenses.

5. In grade seven, students would begin taking basic classes in their specialties based on the results of their career inventory and their strengths assessment. This would include but by no means be limited

to electrician, plumber, health technology, automotive repair, brick mason, and air traffic controller. For example, since New York has a shortage of air traffic controllers, they are recruiting high school graduates who will spend 3 months in training before being placed on the job with an average salary of $102,200.00 (Bennett, 2008). I argue such a program should have been in place beforehand to train the students during high school. The training would have been done through New York air traffic controllers department. These students would receive their diplomas as well as a job as a New York air traffic controller. And the plus for New York is workers would have been trained to specification so that retraining or reprogramming would not be necessary.

6. Students would continue to take reading, math, and technology classes through grade twelve; however, these classes would relate their academic subjects to their careers. Their reading, math and technology classes would be taught by their regular classroom teachers, and their career awareness and development classes would be taught by their school counselors. The work done in the classroom would be distinctly related to the world of work.

7. School and business owners would form a partnership to develop an Apprenticeship Program that would consist of the business owners teaching students in their area of specialty. The master (business owner/ trainer) would make use of on the job training, shadowing, role playing, and simulation. Bailey's & Merritt's article in Centerfocus (1993), "Youth Apprentice: Lessons from the U.S. Experience," identified four basic components of a youth apprenticeship model. This model consists of the following: first, it is designed to be an integral part of the basic education of a broad cross-section of students; second, it integrates academic and vocational instruction; third, it combines classroom and on-the job instruction; fourth, it culminates in recognized and accepted credentials. Catherine Madden, a Detroit-based analyst for research firm Global Insight, "Skilled labor is very important to the process. "I would say (labor) was near the top of the list of items that are very significant factors in determining a location (Maki, 2007)."

8. Assessment of students' progress would be done using traditional (standardized) as well as alternative (performance and portfolio)

assessments. The traditional testing would be utilized for reading and math skills and the performance and portfolio would be used to assess career training status. My rationale for incorporating several assessments is the following: (1) This would allow for a detailed picture of the total student and his or her abilities. (2)The traditional assessment is to increase learning and to pin-point weaknesses and strengths. (3) The performance assessment would allow for higher-level thinking, problem solving skills, allow for emphasis on real-world applications, and focus on the processes the students use to produce their product (French, 2003). (4) This approach would help eliminate the three types of standardized testing biases(bias in testing procedures, bias in test use and bias in content) that detract from validity (Linn & Miller, 2005). Meanwhile, assessments (standardized and performance) would be administered throughout the school year. The passing of exit exams (standardized and performance) would serve as one of the components requirement for graduation. Students would be required to take an exam based upon his or her area of specialty and academic skills.

9. If students successfully pass exit exams, upon graduation, not only would they receive a diploma, but they would be prepared to walk into a job based on their six years of training.

Listed below are the positive outcomes of this curriculum:
1. Students will be an expert in their field because of the length of their training. Starting young is a big plus. Tiger Woods was given a golf club at two years of age. Serena and Venus Williams began their tennis lessons at nine years of age. John Smith, my electrician's son, at the age of 8 began shadowing his father. At the age of 16, he is able to do various types of electrical tasks.
2. Students would be highly motivated to attend school because they could see, feel, hear and taste a bright future.
3. The community would greatly benefit because of the highly skilled workers who would be produced through this curriculum.
4. Parents would support their children if they believe their son or daughter would walk from high school to a productive job.
5. Our many skilled workers would attract big businesses to our city. Furthermore, many of our skilled workers would have the knowledge and motivation to start their own businesses.

6. The businesses involved in the training of our students would be able to have qualified, skilled workers who have already been trained by them.

I highly recommend that this program be tested in certain schools, especially those schools with students experiencing a great deal of academic difficulty and high dropout rate.

Conclusion

The concerns that were previously described along with some possible solutions are just a beginning. In the last 30 years, I have seen many million dollar programs come and go without producing the results of helping our children master the necessary skills needed to financially take care of themselves and their families. I have witnessed our teachers and administrators placed under a tremendous amount of pressure because of factors (attendance, lack of basic supplies, inappropriate school apparel, homework, inappropriate morals and values that are brought from home) that they had no control over. The ideas that I previously mentioned are simply for our children to master the basic skills of reading, writing and math so that they may have an **opportunity** to become productive citizens of our United States. It takes a village to raise children, and the foundation of any village is the families who make up that village. There have always been programs to improve the teaching strategies, the knowledge base, and the curriculum. However, I have never witnessed an extremely aggressive parental program with teeth. Parents are not held accountable for the education of their children.

America is known for being the Land of Opportunity. People from all over the world, in some cases risking their lives, come here to be part of the prosperity that our great nation has to offer. They do this because they know that this is the one place that offers the opportunity to work up to full potential and live out the "Rags to Riches Story". Without skills and knowledge, you take away a child's greatest opportunity of a lifetime which denies the dream of living in America.

References

Aarons, D. I. (2007, June 10a). Black eye for blue ribbon. *The Commercial Appeal*, pp. V1, V3.

Aarons, D. I. (2007, December 19b). Schools audit faults attitude. *Germantown & Collierville Appeal, pp.A1, A5.*

Bailey, T. & Merritt, D. (1993 July) Youth apprentice: lessons from the U.S. experience. *Center Focus,1.*

Bailey, T. & Merritt, D. (1997 October 28). School-to-work for the college. *Education Week, 17(42),9.*

Barber, L. W. & McClellan, M.C. (1987). Looking at America's dropout: Who are they? *Phi Delta Kappan, 69, 264-267.*

Barton, P. (2006). The dropout problem: Losing ground. *Educational Leadership, 63 (5), 14-18.*

Baumrind, D. (1991). The influence of parenting style on adolescent competence and substance use. *Journal of Early Adolescence*, 11(1), 56-95.

Bennett, C. (2008, July 14). FAA kids are in 'control'. *New York Post* Retreived October 23, 2009, from http://www.nypost.com/p/news/regional/faa_kids_are_in_control_02…

Berndt, T. (1999). Friends' influence on students' adjustment to school. *Educational* Psychologist, 34, 15-28.

Black, S. (2002). The well-rounded student. *American School Board Journal*, 189(6), 33-35.

Clay, B. & Johnson, W. (2008 September). Motivating and inspiring African American male to achieve. *Black Star Project*, *1*.

Carr, Richard W. (2009, August). A call to arms for believers: The battle for Memphis youth. *Juvenile Intervention & Faith-Based Follow-Up (JIFF)*. Retreived August 19, 2009, from http://www. jiffyouth.org/calltoarms.htm.

Carson, B., & Murphey, C. (1990). *Gifted hands.* Grand Rapids: Zondervan Publishing House.

Choa, R.K. (2000). Cultural explanations for the role of parenting in the school success of Asian American children. In R.D. Taylor & M.C. Wang (EDS), *Resilience across contexts: Family, work, culture, and community.* Mahwah, NJ: Lawrence Erlbaum.

Choi, Y.E., Bempechat, J., & Ginsburg, H.P. (1994). Educational socialization in Korean American children: A Longitudinal study. *Journal of Applied Developmental Psychology: Special Issue: Diversity and Development of Asian Americans, 15(3), 313-318.*

Christenson, S.L. (2004). The family-school partnership: An opportunity to promote the learning competence of all students. *School Psychology Review*, 33(1), 83-104.

Denton, K., & West, J. (2002). *Children's reading and math achievement in kindergarten and first grade.* Washington, DC: National Center for Education Statistics.

Education Act 1996. Retrieved May 23, 2009 from *Newcastle Children's Services.* Web site: http://www.newcastle.gov.uk/core.

Farr, M., Ludden, L. & Shatkin, L. (2003). *300 Best jobs without a four-year degree.* Indianapolis, IN: JIST Works.

Farr, M. (2009). *Top 100 career without a four-year degree.* **Indianapolis, IN: JIST Works.**

French, D. (2003). **A new vision of authentic assessment to overcome the flaws in high-stakes testing.** *Middle School Journal,* 35(1), 1423.

Garcia, D. (2004). **Exploring connections between the construct of teacher efficacy and family involvement practices: Implications for urban teacher preparation.** *Urban Education,* **39(3), 290-315.**

Gardner, Howard (1983). *Frames of Mind: The theory of multiple intelligences.* **New York: Basic Books.**

Gardner, Howard (1993). *Multiple intelligences: The theory in practice.* **New York:** Basic Books.

Gardner, Howard (2000). *Intelligence reframed: Multiple intelligences for the 21ˢᵗ Century.* **New York: Basic Books.**

Gewertz, C. (2006). **H.G. dropouts say lack of motivation top reason to quit.** *Education,* 25(26), 1, 14.

Goetz, K. (2007, October 30). **Cheap eats, courtesy of MCS catering,** *The Commercial Appeal,* **pp. A1, A3.**

Goyette, K., & Xie, Y. (1999). **Educational expectations of Asian American youths: Determinants of ethnic differences.** *Sociology of Education,* 72(1), 22-36.

Harris, S., Lowery, S. (2002). A view from the classroom. *Educational Leadership,* **59(8), 64-65.**

Hoyt, K.B. (1981*) Career education: Where it is and where it is going?* **Salt Lake City, Utah: Olympus Publishing Co.**

Huntsinger, C. S., Jose, P.E., & Larsen, S.L. (1998). Do parent practices to encourage academic competence influence the social adjustment of young European American and Chinese American children? *Developmental Psychology*, 34,747-756.

Individuals with Disabilities Education Act of 1997. Pub.L. No. 105-17. C.F.R. 3000 (1997).

Individuals with Disabilities Education Act of 2004. Pub.L. No. 108-446. (2004).

Jacobsen, D. (2003). *Philosophy classroom teaching: Bridging the gap* (2nd ed.) Upper Saddle River, NJ: Prentice Hall.

Kazis, R. & Goldberger, S.(1995). *The role of employers: The integration of work-based learning.* New York: Teachers College Press.

Kober, N, (2006). *A public education primer: Basic (and sometimes surprising) facts about the U. S. education system.* Washington, DC: Center on Education Policy.

Kohl, G.O., Lengua, L.J., & McMahon, R.J. (2000). Parent involvement in school: Conceptualizing multiple dimensions and their relations with family and demographic risk factors. *Journal of School Psychology*, 38(6), 501-523.

Kumar, R.B. (2005, July 12). Board surprised KIPP so costly: Memphis pays $1 million a year. *The Commercial Appeal*, p. B2.

Lee, E. (1997). *Chinese American families. Working with Asian Americans: A guide for clinicians.* New York: Guilford.

Linn, R.L., & Miller, M.D. (2005). *Measurement and assessment in teaching (9th ed.).* Upper Saddle River, NJ: Pearson.

Lowell, G. (1989). Lowell City Magnet School: The Microsociety. *Phi Delta Kappan*, 71, 136-138.

Lynch, R.L., & Harnish, D. (1998). *Preparing pre-service teacher education* students *to use work-based strategies to improve instruction. In contextual teaching and learning: Preparing teachers to enhance student success in the workplace and beyond.* Columbus, OH: ERIC Clearing house on Adult, Career, and Vocational Education, Center on Education and Training Employment and Washington, DC: ERIC clearinghouse on teaching and Teacher Education American Association of Colleges for teacher Education.

Maki, A. (2007, March 1). Tupelo had edge in 3 areas—Skilled labor, air quality, politics won Toyota over. *The Commercial Appeal,* p. B6.

Management issues at MCS. (2007, December 17). *The Commercial Appeal, p.A6.*

Memphis City Schools, Memphis, Tennessee, Department of Federal Programs, Grants & Compliance-Title I Schools (2009, December). Retrieved December 13, 2009, from Memphis City Schools Web site: http://www.mcsk12.net/aboutmcs-nclb-tis.asp.

Moncarz, R. & Crosby, O. (2004-2005,Winter). Job outlook for people who don't have a bachelor's degree. *Occupational Outlook Quarterly.* Retreived December 13, 2009, from http://www.bls.gov/opub/ooq/2005/winter/art.

Morrison, C. (2009, May 21). Tenn. Mom jailed for truant second-grader: Woman sentenced to 2 days behind bars. *The Commercial Appeal,* p.B5.

McDevitt, T., & Ormrod, J. (2007). *Child development and education (3ʳᵈ ed.)* Upper Saddle River, NJ: Merrill/Prentice Hall.

National Center for Education Statistics. (2005). *The condition of education 2005.* Washington, DC: U.S. Department of Education.

No Child Left Behind Act of 2001. *Public Law 107-110* (8 January 2002). Washington, DC: U.S. Government Printing Office.

Oakes, L. (2005). *Keeping track: How schools structure inequality (2ⁿᵈ ed.)* New Haven, CT: Yale University Press.

Okagaki, L., & Frensch, R.A. (1998). Parenting and children's achievement: A multiethnic perspective. *American Educational Research Journal, 35,* 123-144.

Piaget, J. (1970). *The science of education and the psychology of the child.* New York: Orion Press.

Perrusquia, M., & Goetz, K. (2007, December 17). No-bid school contracts no panacea. *The Commercial Appeal,* pp. A1, A8.

Public plays the chump. (2009, April 21). *The Commercial Appeal,* p.A8.

Richmond, E. (2009, October 18). Why so many aren't ready. *Las Vegas Sun,* pp. 1, 8, 9.

Riley, R. (2008). *Great careers with a high school diploma.* New York: Infobase Publishing.

Ripley, A. (2008, December 8). Can she save our school? *Time Magazine,* 172 (23), pp. 36-44.

Roberts, J. (2006, January 20). Big employers seek more qualified workers—forum sees middle schools as key to message: Don't mess up. *The Commercial Appeal, p. A1*

Roberts, J. (2008, October 25a). MCS grad rates decline: District falls farther from federal guideline. *Germantown & Collierville Appeal, pp. A1, A4.*

Roberts, J. (2008, August 5b). City school plan on table. *The Commercial Appeal,* pp. A1, A10.

Roberts, J. (2009, March 14a). Hamilton High fight could be connected to area feud. *Local New The Commercial Appeal,* pp.B1, B2.

Roberts, Jane. (2009, May 12b). Schools'cell use on hold. *Germantown & Collierville Appeal, pp. A1, A3.*

Rosemond, J. (2008, June 12). Teachers need backup from parents if the system is to work. *The Commercial Appeal,* p.M3.

Shane, S. & Fernandez, M. (2009, May 27). A Judge's own story highlights her mother *The New York Times.* Retrieved May 28, 2009, from http://www.nytimes.com/2009/05/28/lus/politics/28mother.html?hpw.

Stern, D. (1995). *Employer options for participation in school-to-work programs.* Washington, DC: Brookings Institution.

Swanson, C. (2004). *The real truth about low graduation rates: An evidence-based commentary.* Washington, DC: Urban Institute. Retrieved March 30, 2006 from http://www.urban.org.

Swanson, C. (2006). Bigger district size gives superintendents earnings edge. *Education Week,* 25 (43), 18-19.

Taylor, B. (1993). An investigation of a career education project for African American elementary students in an urban setting (*Doctorial dissertation,* Kansas State University, 1993).

Tennessee Department of Education Accountability Division State Report 2007. Retrieved December 29, 2007, from http://tennesse.gov/education/.reportcard/index.shtml.

Tennessee Department of Education Accountability Division State Report 2008. Retrieved December 29, 2008, from http://tennesse.gov/education/.reportcard/index.shtml.

Tompkins, G. (2006). *Literacy for the 21st century: A balanced approach* (4th ed.). Upper Saddle River, NJ: Merrill/Prentice Hall.

Waldron, C. (2008, August 4). Judge Greg Mathis on making the right choice: You have to determine what you want your life to be {Interview with Judge Greg Mathis}. *Jet Magazine, 114 (4) 42-46.*

Watson, M. (2003, February 2). Hot list of project sites snubs Memphis. *The Commercial Appeal, p. B7*

Unger, H.G. (2006). *But what if I don't want to go to college? A guide to success through alternative education.* *(3th ed.).*New York: Infobase Publishing.

U.S. Department of Education. (2001). *The longitudinal evaluation of school change and performance (LESCP) in Title I schools: Final report.*
Washington, D.C.: Author

U.S. Department of Education, Office for Civil Rights.(2009). *Protecting students with disabilities.* Retrieved from http://www. ed.gov/about/offices/list/ocr/504faq.html.

U.S. Department of Labor (2007). Bureau of Labor Statistics. Retrieved May 15, 2007 , from http://www.bls.gov/opub/.

U.S. Newswire (2009). *News report reveals that 75% of young Americans are unfit for military services.* Retrieved November 5, 2009 from http:// news.aol.com/article/new-report-reveals-that-75percent-of/75...

Vergos, J. (2007, June 21). Time for a school takeover. *The Memphis Flyer, p.17.*

The End

LaVergne, TN USA
08 June 2010
185396LV00004B/223/P